MORE THAN AN
OPERA HOUSE

Contributing and Managing Editor: James S. Murray
Designer: Warren Penney

Published by Lansdowne Press, Sydney
a division of RPLA Pty Limited
176 South Creek Road, Dee Why West, N.S.W., Australia, 2099.
First published 1983
© Copyright The Sydney Opera House Trust
Produced in Australia by the Publisher
Typeset in Australia by Walter Deblaere & Associates
Printed by Tien Mah Litho Printing (Pte) Ltd
2, Jalan Jentera, Jurong, Singapore

National Library of Australia Cataloguing-in-Publication Data

Hubble, Ava Temperley.
More than an opera house.

Includes index.
ISBN 0 7018 1723 2.

1. Sydney Opera House (Sydney, N.S.W.).
I. Title.

725'. 822'099441

All rights reserved. Subject to the Copyright Act 1968, no
part of this publication may be reproduced, stored in a
retrieval system, or transmitted in any form, or by any means,
electronic, mechanical, photocopying, recording, or otherwise,
without the prior written permission of the publisher.

MORE THAN AN
OPERA HOUSE

AVA HUBBLE

LANSDOWNE
Sydney Auckland London New York

Contents

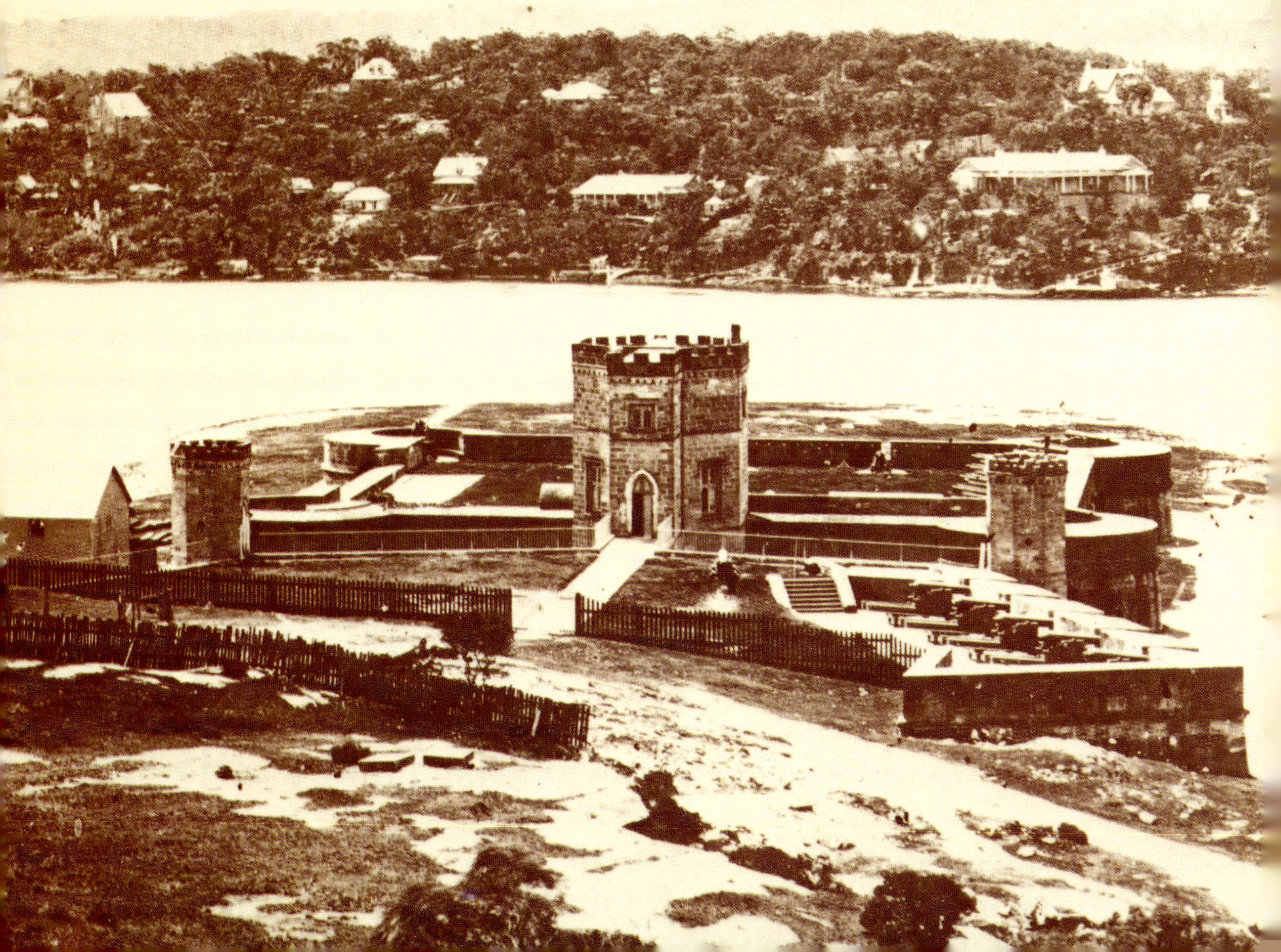

AN OPTICAL ILLUSION

An external view

The rising towers of the central city, seen framed between the sail roofs of the Opera House, all creative works of man.

The Opera House always seems to be photographed dazzling in the sunshine, against the fresh nautical splash of the harbour. Yet the building looks just as enchanting when seen emerging through the grey of an early morning mist, or, better still, standing out with majestic integrity against the blackest storm, as lightning rips the sky.

The atmosphere at the Opera House also changes like the weather. At night there is excitement and romance in the air as patrons, many of them glamorously dressed, arrive for pre-theatre dinner and performances. But when the bustle in the foyers and forecourt subsides and performances begin, you can walk around the promenade and easily imagine yourself at a holiday resort, or aboard a cruise ship and thousands of miles from the crowds and stresses of city life. By ten pm there will be more hubbub. If you return to the building then, you can watch the closing scenes of performances on closed-circuit television in the foyers, and hear the rising tide of applause and cries of "bravo!" emanating from the theatres. Suddenly exit doors are flung open and you are engulfed by the audience, hundreds of patrons, intent on being the first to board a Park & Ride bus, catch a taxi, secure a supper table, or be first in a queue for autographs.

Long after the stars have driven away to their hotels or late night parties at the homes of admirers, young lovers and other strollers can be seen meandering around the promenade. With the pink light of dawn tugs chug out to the heads to assist the liners and container vessels to reach their berths around the harbour, and the first shift of cleaners arrives to help groom the Opera House for the coming day. Joggers follow, circling the promenade alone or in packs or pairs. The city's life is quickening, flotillas of ferries and hydrofoils head determinedly for Circular Quay and serene yachts prove that even the skippers of pleasure craft can be early risers. Not all of the billowing canvas is white; many of the sails are bright red or yellow. Some are candy-striped.

At seven a.m. Opera House security staff change shifts. The senior's first task at the gatehouse is to see that the Australian Flag and the

Looking down on the north-west corner of the promenade from the northern foyer of the Concert Hall. The descending sun casts human shadows.

Left. In dark silhouette against the setting sun, the Opera House appears devoid of life.

9

Opera House pennants are aloft in the forecourt. The flags of other nations also fly there on their national days.

Whenever the weather is fine one elderly Sydneysider always begins his day at the Opera House. With his morning paper and 'a bucket of coffee' he sits reading and enjoying the harbour scenes before his constitutional. He arrives about eight am. With a towel he mops up the dew on his favourite bench, facing the International Shipping Terminal.

Most rehearsals begin at ten am, but musicians and other artists often arrive much earlier to breakfast in the Green Room. Musicians walk quickly to the stage door, rarely stopping to enjoy sunshine or sea breezes in case the salt air seeps into their instrument cases and warps precious violins and cellos. Shabbily dressed people are also seen at this time of day wandering around the building, a reminder of hard times.

By nine am tourists, many of them exotically clothed in saffron robes, saris, stetsons and turbans, are setting off on the first guided tour of the day. Well-organized Japanese visitors arrive by the coachload and bound up the monumental staircase to photograph each other posed against the backdrop of the building and the Harbour Bridge. Tickets for

A tour guide reveals the mysteries of John Olsen's mural, Salute to Five Bells, while the tourists relax on the steps of the north foyer. The pattern of girders supports the huge windows.

The Harbour Restaurant caters for lovers of the open air. At times outdoor entertainment enlivens the scene, performed on an improvised stage nearby.

guided tours are sold at ground level, in the foyer which also serves as an entrance to the Exhibition Hall, Library and Cinema.

The self-service Harbour Restaurant on the promenade does not open until eleven am, but champagne breakfasts are served on special occasions. A breakfast of bacon and eggs, sausages, tomatoes, baked beans and rolls, washed down with champagne, orange juice and coffee was served on February 24, 1978 when thousands began arriving on the promenade just after dawn to welcome the liner Queen Elizabeth II, as she sailed into Sydney for the first time; and breakfast is always served on Anzac Day — April 25 — when thousands of ex-servicemen come into the city for the Dawn Service at the Cenotaph in Martin Place.

The Harbour Restaurant, which has indoor and outdoor tables, also stays open until the early hours of the morning on such special occasions as New Year's Eve and the Opera House's birthday — October 20 — when a dance floor is set up on the promenade nearby and visitors are invited to waltz and dance the can-can and the conga. There have been times when the conga line has been seen weaving its exuberant way around the entire circumference of the building.

Overleaf. Like tabernacles of delight, the glass faces of the Opera House suggest hospitality, entertainment, even mystery, as the lights delineating the highest points defeat the surrounding darkness.

11

From 1975 until 1981 a free outdoor party to celebrate New Year's Eve and the commencement of the January Festival of Sydney was presented at the Opera House. A stage was set up on the front steps for these annual concerts which featured the chorus and principals of the Australian Opera, the Elizabethan Sydney Orchestra and stars of The Australian Ballet, light entertainment and rock and pop. Meanwhile, jazz bands, pop, rock and reggae groups and marimba orchestras played around the promenade for those who preferred to dance rather than attend the concert in the forecourt. There were champagne bars and port-a-loos, fireworks and Auld Lang Syne at midnight. Alas! The antics of a few beer can and bottle throwing hooligans among the vast crowd of revellers proved so dangerous that the New Year's Eve parties were suspended. Similar antics also put a stop to the free rock concerts which were once a regular outdoor attraction. The spectacle of as many as one hundred thousand young people jumping up and down with exhilaration as their idols played on a stage set up in the forecourt was among the most rewarding ever seen at the Opera House; but when Doc Neeson, of The Angels, was injured on stage by a flying wine flagon during the New Year's Eve gala of 1980, the shows came to an end. Similar incidents at Sunday afternoon performances had threatened the safety of artists, audiences and staff several times previously.

Happily, dancing on the promenade remains part of the management's regular outdoor family entertainment on Sundays. Sunday is the time when thousands of Sydneysiders join tourists for a leisurely day around the Opera House. Family parties begin arriving with their picnic baskets from early in the morning. They stroll round the deck, bask in the sun and read the Sunday papers. Others wander away to visit the neighbouring Botanic Gardens and the taverns, art galleries and curio shops in the historic Rocks area of town. Before lunch and the afternoon's entertainment begins, there are Opera House exhibitions to visit, backstage and front-of-house tours, free chamber music concerts in the Recording Hall and stacks of brochures to collect. Sometimes a regatta enlivens the day on the harbour. The Great Ferry boat Race, part of the Festival of Sydney, attracts huge crowds to vantage points around the Opera House. The ferries, festooned with bunting, line up awaiting the starter's orders under the bridge, on handicaps according to age. The older vessels set off first. They must run to the heads and back. As the boats near the finishing line there is a deafening cheering from shore and deck.

The Sunday afternoon programmes outdoors are presented in the forecourt and around the deck between noon and sunset. As many as four different shows may be presented simultaneously, but there is no great pomp and circumstance. Visitors may like to stand watching the gymnasts or karate experts in the forecourt, or they may prefer to

Patriotic marching girls enliven the promenade. The Opera House outdoors attracts large throngs, the entertainment as varied as the more serious arts within.

The Concert Hall and the Opera Theatre demand a certain athleticism as they are both approached by massive stairs. The aerial effect, however, is worth the effort.

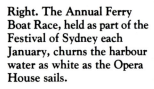

Right. The Annual Ferry Boat Race, held as part of the Festival of Sydney each January, churns the harbour water as white as the Opera House sails.

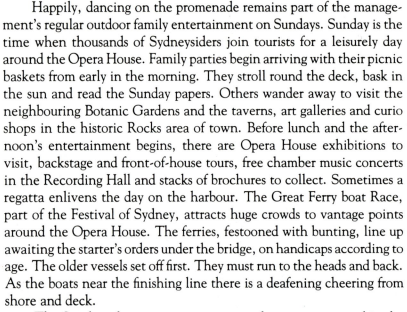

wander on, lingering later to listen to a bush band or a brass band. There will be puppet shows, capering clowns, marching girls and strolling minstrels, and perhaps some square-dancing or traditional dances presented by magnificently costumed new settlers. The afternoon's programme always ends with dancing to the music of a Dixieland jazz band outside the Harbour Restaurant. There will be more outdoor entertainment on public holidays, a mad hatters' parade at Easter, and the Shell National Folkloric Festival, which is presented in Opera House theatres in June each year, traditionally begins with a Saturday afternoon procession from Circular Quay and a pageant of national music and dancing in the forecourt. The Opera House has become the focus for carnival processions — and even protest marches — and the starting or finishing line of cross-country motor and cycle tours and marathon runs.

Thousands of children visit the Opera House for schools' concerts and the Babies' Proms. This series is presented in the Recording Hall The tiny tots sit on mats on the floor listening to nursery music and classical pops. They clap along and hop, skip and march about in time with the music too. The conductor often hands over his baton to one of the children and during every concert the orchestra's timpanists are temporarily replaced by a succession of ambitious young drummers and cymbalists. The proms always end with general mingling and an

Children, and others, enjoy the antics of a clown on the forecourt with a cruise liner as backdrop.

Right. The Annual Folkloric Festival attracts a multi-cultural crowd to watch dancers from Oceania and distant Africa.

A Malay girl, supple and controlled, gyrates to the emotive rhythms of tropical South-East Asia.

A Balinese dancer, employing intricate eye and hand movements, reveals the mysteries of the Ramayana.

exchange of musical thoughts and ideas. During school holidays there are free story readings in the foyers and introductory programmes like Getting To Know About Ballet, which are presented in rehearsal studios backstage. Schoolchildren and romping tiny tots often picnic on the promenade or in the gardens with their parents or teachers. City workers visit the Opera House for the Lunchtime Happenings — free series of concerts, travel films and seminars in the Cinema. They bring packed lunches to eat in the theatre during the programmes, which start at one-ten pm and end at one-fifty pm.

The men and women who work in the ground floor offices sit with their backs to the windows and the temptations and distractions outside. The only time they feel themselves better off is during stormy weather. When thunder rolls, even the most resolute are drawn to the windows to watch the wind and rain thrash the harbour into a fury. Traffic banks up on the bridge and drenched tourists make for the shelter of the Harbour Restaurant, their umbrellas often turned inside out by the force of the gale. Perhaps there will be rainbows and serene skies later — a reminder of Beethoven's Pastoral Symphony of thanksgiving after the storm.

IN THE WINGS

How the Opera House began

Left. The vertebrae of the first sails rise above the podium. Above, a construction worker welds metal skeletons around which the great building will rise.

W hat about the amusing incidents backstage? "There must be hundreds of funny stories about the Opera House," people insist. But, as yet, there is no vast repertoire of amusing anecdotes. The building's long history of planning and construction provoked only controversy and bitterness. Even in 1972, when the complex was nearing completion and with the official opening by Queen Elizabeth only a year away, the media was still mainly interested in costs, controversy and more controversy.

In 1972 the final cost of the Opera House was being estimated at $100 million — a sum that would have the buying power of $300 million in 1983 — and it was in 1972 that it was revealed that the complex would not have a car park. Earlier, it had been announced that the new opera, Rites of Passage, by the Australian composer, Peter Sculthorpe, which had been commissioned for the official opening performance, would not be completed in time.

In 1972 stage-struck front-of-house and other staff were being engaged to help prepare for the commencement of performances at the Opera House. They may have joined up wildly excited at the prospect of one marvellous production after another, and by thoughts of the arrival of star artists and visiting royalty. But enthusiasm soon waned.

If you were on the staff of the Opera House in those days — particularly if you were a member of the publicity department — you often felt as though you were working as an apologist for a corrupt building contractor, rather than as an assistant in a glamorous theatre.

The press was particularly savage and sneering. Most of the shock stories were true, of course. It was senseless to deny them. The easiest way out for new Opera House staff was to blame someone else and refer reporters to the Department of Public Works which was responsible for overseeing the construction of the building.

By the beginning of 1973 the final cost of the Opera House was being estimated at $101 million. A few months later, during test performances, the media discovered that you could not see the stage from some of the seats in the Opera Theatre!

Peter Sculthorpe, the contemporary Australian composer, is well known for his imaginative works.

But there was good news too. The acoustics were finding approval. The Cleveland Orchestra had been signed up. There would be a substitute for a car park — a Park & Ride Service for Opera House patrons. Only 98 of the 1,547 seats in the Opera Theatre had a "restricted view" of the stage.

But the media did not seem interested in positive news. "Seats you cannot see from to be sold cheaply to blind people," was a newspaper story which encouraged the widespread belief that the Opera House would prove the world's most expensive white elephant.

Morale suffered. Most of the staff engaged at the Opera House in 1972 and 1973 were young — many of them too young to have vivid memories of the trauma in Sydney in 1966 when the Danish architect of the complex, Jørn Utzon, resigned and left Australia.

Jørn Utzon.

Many newly-appointed staff began to wonder if they had made a mistake. As you became more aware of the Opera House's heart-breaking history of construction and the consequences of many past decisions, you could understand the widespread contempt for everyone associated with the management of the complex.

It was warranted, you often felt — the accusation inherent in every critic's query about costs and limitations — Opera House staff were just another coterie of self-seeking bureaucrats, intent on glossing over the fact that a masterpiece had been used as a political whipping-boy — and become maimed in the process.

That process had begun with Eugene Goossens, an English composer and conductor of Belgian descent, who had arrived in Australia for the first time in 1947. He was fifty-four and came to take up the appointments of chief conductor of the Sydney Symphony Orchestra and director of the New South Wales State Conservatorium of Music. He arrived with a splendid reputation. Previously he had been conductor of the Cincinatti Symphony Orchestra and a regular guest conductor with the world's leading orchestras and opera companies. He was the first chief conductor of the Sydney Symphony Orchestra, which was formed in 1946, and was the first of the Australian Broadcasting Commission's six state symphony orchestras to be established — to replace the commission's original, much smaller concert ensembles.

Eugene Goossens.

Many people wondered why the distinguished Goossens had agreed to come and work in the Antipodes. It was rumoured that his total salaries and allowances as chief conductor of the Sydney Symphony Orchestra and director of the Sydney conservatorium exceeded the income of the Australian prime minister of the day, Ben Chifley. At any rate, local musicians and administrators considered themselves lucky to get Goossens at any price. As soon as he arrived he announced that he wanted to make the Sydney Symphony Orchestra one of the six best orchestras in the world.

Right. The New South Wales State Conservatorium of Music is built into the old stables of Governor Macquarie's proposed Government House.

Below. The Sydney Symphony Orchestra was formed in 1946 by the Australian Broadcasting Commission. The orchestra has 96 members. Sir Charles Mackerras was appointed the orchestra's chief conductor in 1981, the first Australian to hold the position. Previous chief conductors of the orchestra were Eugene Goossens, Nicolai Malko, Dean Dixon, Moshe Atzmon, Willem van Otterloo and Louis Fremaux.

Goossens, whose compositions include operas, was taken aback to discover there was no theatre suitable for first class opera in Sydney and he began complaining to associates about the lack of an opera theatre. In 1949 he conducted his own opera, Judith, at the Sydney Conservatorium, with a young stenographer, Joan Sutherland, in the title role. It was following this performance that Goossens later began lobbying vigorously for a new opera house for the city.

Initially, he attacked the then general manager of the Australian Broadcasting Commission, Charles (later Sir Charles) Moses. The long-suffering Moses was sympathetic, but he was not in the position to commission a new opera house — and he was very busy administering the national broadcaster. At the time Moses' work included collaborating with Bernard Heinze to establish ABC symphony orchestras in all states. But Goossens persisted. "He used to get very heated," Moses recalls.

By 1952 Moses became so worn down by Goossens' attacks, that he arranged for the conductor to discuss the matter of a new opera house with the premier, Mr Cahill. That first encounter between the wary, tough little Labor politician and the highly-cultivated, passionately-determined musician was not successful.

Cahill, who had battled his way through the Great Depression, had more urgent priorities — housing for ex-servicemen, the building of schools, hospitals and new highways. In any case, the premier thought his government was doing quite enough to support Goossens' interests in funding the Sydney conservatorium and providing an annual subsidy for the new Sydney Symphony Orchestra.

The rebuff infuriated the conductor. At every opportunity he derided the premier to reporters and scoffed at Cahill's failure to appreciate that a city was no city without an opera house. In spite of, or because of those attacks, Cahill reconsidered the matter. As we know, he eventually became as eager about the project as Goossens himself. In fact, once convinced of the desirability of an opera house, you would have thought the idea Cahill's alone!

The premier also took full advantage of Goossens' expertise and experience. He appointed the conductor to the four-man committee established to advise his government on "how to go about building an opera house". Goossens was also closely associated with the premier's committee of three architects who selected the site of the building.

A site over the underground Wynyard Railway Station in the city was one originally put forward as a possible location. Incidentally, trains were Goossens' great hobby. When touring to country districts with the Sydney Symphony Orchestra, he would usually insist on travelling in the engine-driver's cabin. His daughters, Sidonie and Rene, who have settled in Australia, recall their father at home, playing recordings of

Sir Charles Moses.

The Premier, Mr J. J. Cahill.

A view of Bennelong Point from the eastern side of Farm Cove in 1846. In a series of paintings of Government House and Fort Macquarie, the painter, Edward George Peacock transformed the Australian landscape into something softer than its reality.

The fort stands sentinel where the Opera House now cuts the air, and two off-duty soldiers in their regimental red enjoy the scene.

The expected enemy in the 1840's is hard to posit. The French had caused alarm from the beginning of the colony; the Russians and the Chinese would be later bogeys but Fort Macquarie itself would fall, to be replaced by a tram depot built to look like a fort.

trains rattling along the tracks. But despite his passion for the railways, Goossens violently opposed the idea of an opera house above Wynyard Station. He always favoured Bennelong Point. His secretary, Phyllis Williams, remembers the maestro insisting that she take lunchtime walks with him from the conservatorium, through the Botanic Gardens to the point. "This is where it must be," Goossens would insist.

But Premier Cahill had earmarked Bennelong Point as the site of a new international shipping terminal. "NO! NO!" Goossens is reported to have objected. "Put your shipping terminal on the other side."

In 1955, when Bennelong Point was selected as the site, Eugene Goossens was knighted for his services to music in Australia. At the time he was lionized in Sydney. He was revered by members of the orchestra and students at the conservatorium, acclaimed by audiences and music critics, and he and his third wife were constantly besieged with dinner and party invitations by the establishment. Even his musical compositions were well received and extensively publicized by the Australian press. On November 22, 1954 Goossens' epic oratorio, The Apocalypse, a work for two choirs, symphony orchestra, organ and soloists, was given its world premiere at the Sydney Town Hall before a capacity audience, with the composer conducting.

A portrait of Sir Eugene Goossens by the Australian artist, Henry Hanke, painted in 1955. It hangs in the building's Dennis Wolanski Library and Archives of the Performing Arts.

Who would have dreamt that Goossens would soon be at the centre of another apocalyptic event — a disastrous scandal that would force him to leave Sydney a disgraced and broken man? But the incredible happened. On March 9, 1956 Goossens returned to Sydney from engagements as a guest conductor overseas. When he arrived at Sydney airport, Goossens was searched by Customs officers. About a thousand pornographic photographs, films and books described as "indecent" were discovered in his baggage. The depth of the headlines can be imagined; the public's sense of shock was profound.

Following news of the Customs charge, Goossens resigned his Sydney appointments. He had no alternative.

Despite the extent of his achievements in Sydney, few of Goossens' associates stood by him. Sir Charles Moses remembers that he even had difficulty in persuading the Australian Broadcasting Commission's board of directors to follow the normal practice of paying a retiring chief conductor's fare back to his home base.

Other sympathisers have made the point that any material found in the conductor's possession was unlikely to have been as salacious as that freely available in many parts of Australia only a few years later; but in the 1950s the customs laws were so much stricter than in the 1980s and community attitudes more puritanical than now.

At first, Goossens determined to contest the Customs charge. His legal advisers, however, in view of the prevailing censorship laws, feared he might lose the case and be gaoled in consequence. Goossens subsequently offered no defence and on March 22, 1956 he paid a £100 fine. A mere bagatelle. What the offence cost Goossens was his health and his career. On May 26, 1956 the conductor and his wife left Australia on a KLM flight, reportedly incognito as Mr and Mrs E. Gray. He died in England in 1962. He was sixty-nine.

For many years people were inclined to snigger at the very mention of Goossens' name. Today, there is a sense of shame in Sydney about the persecution and possible injustice he met with, and there have been attempts to atone.

Soon after the Opera House opened in 1973, a portrait of Goossens by the Australian artist, Henry Hanke, was hung in the library. More recently, in 1982, a committee of young Sydney Symphony Orchestra subscribers commissioned a bronze bust of the composer-conductor for display in the foyer of the Concert Hall. The bust, by the Australian sculptor, Peter Latona, was paid for with money donated by the public. It was presented to the Opera House by the committee's patron, Sir Charles Moses, following the second Sydney performance of Goossen's oratorio, The Apocalypse, in the Concert Hall on November 13, 1982. During the ceremony, Sir Charles reminded the audience that Sir Eugene Goossens, "Gene", was not only the first chief conductor of the Sydney Symphony Orchestra, but the man who suggested the building of the Opera House in which they were sitting.

But why persist in calling a performing arts centre an Opera House? The explanation seems to be that everyone followed Eugene Goossens's and Premier Cahill's example.

Cahill approved the idea of a performing arts complex. Never-theless, he persisted in referring to the proposed new building as the Opera House originally proposed by Goossens. When the premier died in 1959, his colleagues, the media and, consequently, the public, went on following his lead and referring to the complex as the Opera House. During the stormy years that followed, nobody seemed to have the time or inclination to think of a more suitable alternative — Sydney Performing Arts Centre for example — and in 1973, when the building was nearing completion, politicians and officials decided it was too late for a change of name. So Opera House, or more formally, Sydney Opera House, the building remains.

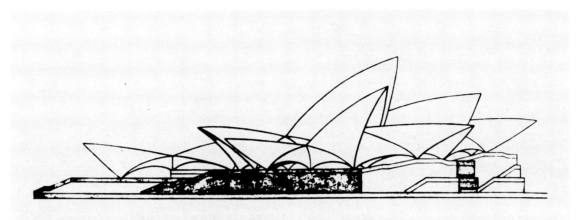

Left. The winning design by Jørn Utzon was later modified by the architect when the engineering difficulties were recognised. The second place went to a group of Philadelphian architects and the London partners, Boissevain and Osmond came third. These designs were much more formal in conception.

In 1957 Jørn Utzon won the international competition commissioned by the New South Wales Government to find a design for the Opera House. The architect was 38 at the time and not widely known. The design contest attracted 233 entries from around the world. Like other entrants, Utzon was, of course, given details of the location of the proposed complex. The site, Bennelong Point, a peninsula on Sydney Harbour, had been chosen by a New South Wales Government committee of three architects who selected the site of the building.

The architect, who had never visited Australia at the time of the contest, said his design was inspired by mental images of "life on Sydney Harbour". Utzon is a keen sailor and his Opera House is often compared to a majestic yacht or a galleon in full sail.

He won the design contest with rough, not detailed plans. "The drawings submitted are simple to the point of being diagrammatic," concluded the international panel of architects who judged the contest. "Nevertheless we have returned again and again to the study of these drawings. We are convinced that they present a concept of an opera house which is capable of being one of the great buildings of the world."

Right. Yachts echo the inanimate sails of the Opera House, and were the 'mental images' in Utzon's mind when planning its design.

Above. Jørn Utzon holidaying in Spain in 1982. The architect has continued to design arresting buildings in many parts of the world but none has achieved the fame of the Opera House.

Initially, however, Utzon's design was not generally acclaimed. There were many Australians who would have preferred a more conventional building, patterned, perhaps, on one of the great European opera houses. But not the New South Wales Premier of the day, J. J. (Joe) Cahill. He was one of the first to champion the Utzon Opera House.

In accordance with the rules of the competition, Utzon's Opera House was, in fact, more than an opera house. His plans were for a performing arts centre, housing, in strict accordance with the competition rules, three theatres: "a large hall to seat between 3,000 and 3,500", suitable for "symphony concerts, including organ music and soloists, large scale opera, ballet and dance, choral", a second hall, seating "about 1,200", for "dramatic presentations, intimate opera, chamber music, concerts, recitals and lectures", and a third, an "experimental theatre".

Utzon's prize as winner of the contest was £5,000 — $10,000 — decimal currency was not introduced in Australia until 1966. £5,000 in 1957 would be the equivalent of $47,000 today.

Above. Four architects judged the Opera House design competition in 1957. From left to right: Cobden Parkes; Professor Leslie Martin; Eero Saarinen, the Finnish-born American architect, and Professor Henry Ingham Ashworth. The judges' decision was not universally popular but it is now widely regarded as an inspired and courageous choice.

Below. The premier, J. J. Cahill, standing beside later and more developed design drawings prepared by Jørn Utzon.

As anticipated, in view of Premier Cahill's enthusiasm for Utzon's design, the architect was also awarded the lucrative commission of directing the construction of the Opera House; but that commission was not part of his prize. The New South Wales Government was not even legally bound to construct the prize-winning entry.

The result of the contest was announced on January 29, 1957 and Utzon arrived in Sydney for the first time six months later. He was tall, blond, handsome and a winner! The press, the public and Premier Cahill were delighted with him. The architect was photographed touring the site of the Opera House — on which a bus station still stood — and photographed in consultation with Cahill — then the minister responsible for construction of the complex.

The castellated tram sheds built on Bennelong Point in 1902. While scores of ferries plied the harbour, trams went long distances into the suburbs from this depot which echoed the former Fort Macquarie. Above right, the tram sheds became a bus station and were finally demolished in 1958 to make way for the Opera House.

Utzon returned home to Denmark after six months of initial discussions. He worked on his plans there for the next five years, with occasional visits to London and Sydney for consultations with the civil engineer, his compatriot, Ove Arup.

Although the architect and Premier Cahill discussed the Opera House extensively in Sydney twice in 1958, following Utzon's 1957 visit, they did not meet again. The premier died suddenly in office on October 19, 1959. The whole course of the Opera House's history of construction might have been very different had the enthusiastic Cahill lived and remained in power. Joe Cahill was widely regarded as a rough-and-tumble Labor politician. There were many who were surprised to find him advocating an opera house and extending support to a then virtually unknown and innovative architect. "He was a man ahead of his time," Utzon said later of Cahill.

Others have said Cahill's interest in the project was motivated by a desire to build a monument to himself. What cannot be disputed is Cahill's sagacity in insisting on the construction of Utzon's building. In the 1950s the very idea of an opera house, let alone an opera house that looked as though "a southerly buster might blow it away", was regarded as mad extravagance in Sydney. Cahill fought bitter opposition about the project from members of his own cabinet, as well as many pillars of the community. "This Opera House will be a burden on the people for all time," said Mr G. Cherry of the Hospitals' Association of New South Wales in October, 1957. "Completely unnecessary," was the opinion of Actors' Equity in January, 1959.

Before his death, Premier Cahill also worked doggedly to find ways and means to raise the money to build the complex. First he set up an appeal fund and later introduced the Opera House Lotteries. Cahill said it would cost £3½ million to build the Opera House — the equivalent of $30 million today. Even in 1957 experts considered the premier's estimate unrealistic — little more than canny, conservative guesswork, designed to counteract his critics' claims that the complex was a luxury New South Wales could not afford.

But undoubtedly Cahill himself, despite the fact that he was the first to predict that the Opera House would ultimately earn dividends for Sydney, would have been shocked by the final cost of something more than $100 million!

Shortly before his death, in spite of the fact that he knew Utzon's plans were far from complete, Cahill began insisting work begin. Test boring on Bennelong Point commenced in 1958 and construction of the foundations began on March 2, 1959.

The Australian architect, Professor Henry Ingham Ashworth, one of the architects who selected the site and a member of the international panel which judged the Opera House design contest, has said he was appalled when construction of the building began before the completion of Utzon's plans. Nevertheless he later reached the conclusion that if construction had not been pushed ahead by an eager premier, Utzon's design would "never have got off the ground".

"In other words," said Ashworth, "if the problems associated with construction had been more widely appreciated earlier, and if it had been suspected, before construction began, that the Opera House would take 14 years and over $100 million to build, Utzon's plans would have been shelved and an alternative design selected by public demand." But in 1958, when the bus station on Bennelong Point was being demolished, excitement began building up in Sydney. Even people who had initially scorned Utzon's design began to look forward to the completion of a glamorous new home for the performing arts in the city.

In 1957 an optimistic Premier Cahill announced that the complex would open on Australia Day, 1963, as part of celebrations marking the 175th anniversary of European settlement.

As the 1950's passed into the 1960's, with Cahill dead and Utzon

Professor H. Ingham Ashworth.

In the pastel shades of dawn or of the fading sun, the curving sails of the building take on a gentler appearance and lose their normally sharper definition.

The Opera House stands on a vast podium built out over Bennelong Point. As the structure took shape, the configurations of the land were lost to view.

in Denmark painstakingly calculating how the roofs of the Opera House could be constructed with absolute confidence, performances in the complex seemed a very distant possibility and anxiety began to mount.

The first controversy broke in 1962 when it was announced that the architect, with the backing of the civil engineer, Ove Arup, had modified the "sail" or "shell" roofs of the building for "aesthetic and structural reasons". The modified plans provided for more space and height in the Opera House and were also reported to enable construction to proceed more quickly, easily and safely. About five years of calculations at the drawing board were necessary before construction of the unique roofs actually began in 1963.

In the same year with the foundations laid, the monumental stairs and podium built, and construction of the roofs — which also form the walls of the complex — about to begin, Utzon, his wife, and their three children came to live in Sydney. Utzon built a home for his family at Palm Beach, a magnificent retreat about 30 kilometres from the city.

'The Vision and the Structure', a series of paintings by Robert Emerson Curtiss, traced the history of construction from July, 1963.

Left. The glass canopies are considered great architectural and construction feats. By day sunlight fills the foyer behind the Opera Theatre, and by night audiences from both the Opera and the Concert Hall have a panoramic view of sea and shore.

Right. Davis Hughes photographed in 1968 with a model of the northern foyer of the Concert Hall.

Sir Malcolm Sargent, the famous English conductor, was impeccable both in dress and musical taste. For him, the arts needed no defence.

Dean Dixon was principal conductor of the Sydney Symphony Orchestra from 1964 to 1967. It is said he was self-conscious about his colour.

The architect's arrival helped to stem the rising tide of criticism and disappointment about the amount of time and money it was taking literally to get the Opera House off the ground.

Professor Ashworth has said that new architectural techniques, of enormous benefit to architecture internationally, were pioneered during the construction of the Opera House. Those techniques were later explained in depth in such books as John Yeoman's Guide to the Sydney Opera House, Harry Sowden's opus about the installation of the huge glass canopies which form the roofs and walls of the major foyers overlooking Sydney Harbour, and Siegfried Giedion's book, Space, Time and Architecture. In the 1960s, however, there were few journalists who took a constructive interest in investigating and explaining the pioneering of new construction techniques at Bennelong Point. The media seemed to exult in the news of rising costs and construction difficulties, yet said little about the astonishing architectural feats, and failed to appreciate that the unique roofs would put Australia on the cultural map and attract huge annual sums in tourist revenue.

"White elephant" was typical of the unchallenged comments published about the Opera House during the construction years. "A joke," the visiting Russian cellist, Edmund Kurtz, was reported as saying. "I do not think they can any longer afford to discuss the cost," condoled the American conductor, Dean Dixon. "I am all for extravagance," said Malcolm Sargent. "It is not that I am against culture but that Opera House has cruelled the fishing," a local angler was quoted as complaining.

Increasingly, the complex became the subject of stories in the international media. Australia was often portrayed as a nation entirely populated by sports lovers who liked a few beers on the side, and who appeared to be quite out of their depth when it came to building opera houses. The Opera House became an embarrassment. By the mid-1960s most Australians regarded the building as an international joke that was tarnishing the country's image. The media cashed in and inevitably the complex became a "political football", as Utzon was to complain.

In 1965, even though the roofs of the building were now soaring skywards, Sydney people travelling by ferry could plainly observe that the Opera House was still far from completion, and that actual performances were well into the future.

That year the Liberal/Country Party coalition, which had been campaigning on a platform of "doing something about the Opera House", swept to power in New South Wales, replacing the long-standing Labor Government which was then headed by Joe Cahill's successor, Jack Renshaw.

"The most stupendous financial bungle," snorted the newly-elected Premier Bob (later Sir Robert) Askin. His Minister of Public Works Davis (later Sir Davis) Hughes, immediately summoned Utzon to his office to account for progress down at Bennelong Point. By then the amazing feat of constructing the exterior of the Opera House was almost complete. Even so, Hughes is reported to have treated Utzon, the protege of his political rivals, with little respect. The new minister talked money and deadlines. He was impatient. Indeed, many of those who elected him to power, wanted more progress and less expense.

Hughes was also reported to be alarmed by the complaints of some of Utzon's associates about the architect's methods of construction and his choice of building materials and sub-contractors.

Utzon remained preoccupied with completing the Opera House to his own exacting standards, even to the design of the knives in the restaurants. Perfection was his goal: hold-ups and expense concerned him less. He is reported to have been more amused than annoyed by the minister's hectoring manner at first; but inevitably, the demanding politician and the uncompromising artist eventually taxed each other's patience to breaking point. On February 26, 1966, after a particularly heated exchange, Utzon verbally resigned in Hughes' office, a decision he later confirmed in writing. The minister accepted his resignation with alacrity and appointed a panel of four Australian architects to complete the Opera House.

The panel was headed by the New South Wales Government Architect, E. H. (Ted) Farmer. Its other members were Peter Hall, from the Government Architect's staff and the man responsible for the interior design of the Opera House as it now stands; and two architects

David Littlemore.

Peter Hall.

in private practice, Lionel Todd and David Littlemore, who were primarily responsible for the preparation of contract documents and day-to-day supervision of construction. These four men faced as mighty a challenge as Franco Alfano, who was asked to complete Turandot on the death of Puccini. They devoted seven years of their lives to completing the Opera House. One of their greatest feats, in concert with the engineer, Ove Arup, was the installation of the huge, billowing glass canopies which form the roofs and walls of the major foyers.

Utzon's supporters, now widely regarded as the enlightened minority, demonstrated in the streets for his reinstatement as sole architect in charge of construction. Among the marchers were Harry Seidler the prominent architect, and an unsuccessful entrant in the design contest, and the distinguished Australian musician, Neville Amadio.

Meanwhile, Utzon instituted legal proceedings against the New South Wales Government for fees he alleged were outstanding for his interior designs for the complex. He was represented by the barrister Neville Wran, who led a New South Wales Labor Government back to power 10 years later.

Utzon's critics have claimed he left incomplete or extremely sketchy designs for the interiors of the building. His detractors have criticised his habit of pondering every detail of design at great length. They have claimed that the Opera House would never have been completed to his satisfaction if he had been allowed to remain in charge. "I wanted the interior to fit the exterior like a walnut in its shell," Utzon has subsequently said.

When he resigned in 1966 most Australians were more relieved than sympathetic. Even those who had some idea of the complexity of the problems associated with construction, thought he had been given "a fair go" — nine years in which to realize his dream.

Following the protests of Utzon's supporters, however, Hughes did invite the architect to reconsider his resignation — but on condition that he work as only one of a panel. Utzon said later, "I did talk to Mr (Peter) Hall about a possible collaboration but I honestly think that was something Davis Hughes did not want." The architect and his family left Australia in May, 1966. Utzon has never returned.

After his departure, bitter controversy was provoked when the new architects proposed major interior design changes which increased the number of theatres in the Opera House from three to five, and involved converting the major multi-purpose theatre into a concert hall. Those design changes were authorized by the government on the recommendation of Davis Hughes in 1967. "They changed their minds about what they wanted inside," Utzon said later.

The decision to remodel the interior is said to have been influenced by the Australian Broadcasting Commission which manages the Sydney

Lionel Todd.

Sir Robert Askin.

Symphony Orchestra. In the mid-1960's the Commission claimed that the Opera House's major, multi-purpose theatre would prove acoustically unsuitable for both symphony concerts and opera. While lobbying for the conversion of the multi-purpose theatre into a concert hall, the Commission also asserted that while symphony concerts had a large following in Sydney, there was not such a large following for opera. That was true enough in 1966, but times change.

Although it has been claimed that Utzon left only sketchy plans for the interior of the Opera House, preliminary work on the major multi-purpose theatre began in the mid-1960's, and by the time Utzon left Sydney in 1966, stage machinery for that theatre had been installed. In 1967, when the proposal to convert the multi-purpose theatre into a concert hall was authorized, that stage machinery was dismantled. It ended up in Long Bay Gaol where it was used for workshop rehabilitation programmes.

In 1967 critics claimed that the conversion of the multi-purpose theatre into a concert hall, and the consequent relegation of opera to the smaller of the two major theatres, would result in a performing arts centre in which opera productions on a grand scale could not be easily accommodated.

That accusation — that an opera house unsuitable for opera had been built at monstrous expense was continually thrown at Opera House staff in the months before the premiere season.

"I cannot be coping . . ." the publicity manager would moan as he slammed down the phone after being interrogated by yet another journalist. "I am just going to weather it out until the end of the first season." "I will just stay until they get the place opened," were typical comments of harried staff in those days. In the meantime, there was plenty of work to be done.

Staff had to learn how to operate the complex's sophisticated stage machinery, the box office, the switchboard, the telex, and the typesetting machine for printing programmes, brochures and posters. Catering staff had to work out how to provide for thousands of patrons, and hundreds of artists and staff simultaneously. The air-conditioning, electric and fire-prevention machinery had to be mastered. Ushers and theatre managers, tour guides, stenographers and security staff were engaged in increasing numbers and everyone had to learn how to find their way around the complex.

One of the first things you discovered about the Opera House was its size: it is much bigger and more beautiful externally than it appears in many photographs.

The building's five theatres seat 5,500 people. There are huge foyer-and-lounge areas, an Exhibition Hall and a Reception Hall. For the uninitiated, finding the way around the building backstage is

The Drama Theatre seats 544 patrons, in straight rows unlike the curving arc of the Opera Theatre seats. Upholstered in vermilion wool, they are of the standard Opera House design.

The Opera Theatre seats 1,547 patrons but 98 box seats only offer a restricted view of the stage. Upholstered in red leather, the seats rest on aluminium frames and are made of white birch plywood.

Right. The Opera House is often deceptive, but its reality is a building of monumental proportions easily rivalling the medieval cathedrals and temples of antiquity.

bewildering. Literally thousands of doors lead into and out of nearly 1,000 separate areas.

The complex houses five rehearsal studios, 40 suites of dressing rooms, ten tuning-up and practice rooms, restaurants, bars and canteens, a library and archive, scenery docks, administration offices, kitchens, pantries, cold-rooms, laundries, wardrobe and wig rooms — and two vast levels below ground, which look like space stations, where massive blocks of air-conditioning and electrical equipment are housed.

In the months leading up to the premiere performances, workmen were still busy completing the building. The maze of concrete corridors backstage had not been signposted, and stairways, corridors and doorways were often blocked by huge rolls of carpet, dressing-tables, stoves, sinks and lavatories awaiting installation. Ladders and paint pots and wheelbarrows piled high with raw materials were other hurdles that impeded your progress as you attempted to negotiate a course from one level to another.

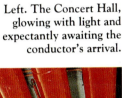

Left. The Concert Hall, glowing with light and expectantly awaiting the conductor's arrival.

Hidden passageways and corridors conceal countless kilometres of piping which carry the air-conditioning to every part of the building.

Staff in their mandatory safety helmets often got lost, sometimes with parties of visiting celebrities and officials who had requested a preview tour of the building. "We are never going to get out," complained a consular wife, as a tearful, newly-appointed tour guide returned yet again to the same dead-end after trying for more than half an hour to escort her party back to the Concert Hall foyer.

"This is a nightmare. It reminds me of the lower decks of a troop ship," exploded the English actor, Robert Morley, lost in the unfinished Opera House with a camera crew and a hapless member of the publicity department. "How would an actor ever find his way back to his dressing room?" demanded Morley, when perspiring and very cross, he was led out of a corridor and into a broom-cupboard.

Until mid-1973 most dressing rooms and rehearsal studios were still under construction and out of bounds but adventurous staff insisted on exploring, and a party of influential visitors once persuaded a guide to include the prohibited area of the dressing rooms in a tour of the complex. After viewing a conductor's suite in which appointments for a sitting room, dressing room and bathroom were still incomplete, the party discovered that the door leading from the suite had either jammed fast, or been locked by a departing foreman.

It was late on a Friday afternoon. Everyone had apparently left for the weekend. At any rate, there was no response to the poundings on the locked door, nor to the visitors' panic-stricken cries for help. Fortunately, there were windows in the suite, though they could not be opened, and a workman was eventually noticed, two levels below, sitting on the unpaved promenade, fishing in Sydney Harbour.

He said he did not hear the banging on the double-glazed windows but something made him look that way, and there were the stranded

Robert Morley, often tongue in cheek, is now best known in Australia for soup advertisements.

tourists, signalling desperately — fearful they would be cooped up in the conductor's suite, with no facilities, until at least Monday morning. There were quite a few similar alarms and rescues. Meanwhile, the instruction from the executive suite was short and sharp: "Get on with it."

The management, the Sydney Opera House Trust, will "engage artists and present some performances", staff were told. "But our job is really to act as a landlord," the briefing continued. "We will hire out the building's theatres to national and state performing companies, and to independent impresarios. They will present most of the programmes. What we have to be do is provide the front-of-house and technical staff, and make sure the Opera House is kept clean and in good working order. We also have to promote the building as a performing arts centre," staff were continually reminded. "It is not a monument. To earn money we have to make sure the Opera House is fully utilized, night and day, throughout the year. When the theatres are not booked for performances or rehearsals, we will hire them out for conventions. We will cater for lunches, fashion parades and wedding receptions in the foyers."

Despite the Opera House's unfortunate image, the theatre lettings department was inundated with enquiries. Indeed, prospective hirers queued up — fledgling companies with plans for pantomimes, business firms booking conventions, seminars and trade displays — charity committees with ideas for exhibitions and musicals.

"They are just going to cash in on the novelty of the place while they can," said a cynic. "They will get their fingers burnt. Who would pay good money to see that?" was the worry of those concerning themselves with "standards". "Is it on ice?" enquired the publicity manager when he was given details of a lieder recital to be presented by a charity committee. "Kitsch," commented the general manager when he was shown a layout for a brochure about the Opera House restaurants and reception facilities. "You ought to know; you are wearing it," snapped the man from the art department. Not everyone lasted the distance. "Amateur night at the Balmain Bijou," publicity staff criticised as they tried to make sense of a trickle that became a torrent of information about the opening season — September 28 to December 31, 1973. The good news was that the major companies — The Australian Opera, The Australian Ballet, the Sydney Symphony Orchestra, The Old Tote Theatre Company, Musica Viva Australia, had all booked theatres for the opening and subsequent seasons. Prokofiev's epic opera, War and Peace, was definitely going to be the first of the premiere season attractions. "So apt," someone lisped.

The impresario, Jack Neary, had signed up Petula Clark, Helen Reddy and Cliff Richard for first season Concert Hall performances. He also intended to present shows starring Carol Burnett, Rod McKuen,

Sir Harry Secombe, these days a shadow of his former self, appears here in more ample days.

Cliff Richard, an evergreen pop star and now born-again Christian, has made many visits to Australia.

Harry Secombe, David Frost and Rolf Harris. Harry M. Miller had been on the phone about another "Sunday Night at the Opera House" series.

There were enquiries from the Dance Company, the International Society of Contemporary Music, the National Film Theatre of Australia, the Marionette Theatre of Australia, and a man who had an idea about disco dancing in the Recording Hall on Friday nights. Obviously there was going to be "a lot on for young people".

"This is the people's Opera House," became the catchcry — even the juniors kept repeating that. "We must cater for everybody" was the order. "We must make sure as wide a range of attractions as possible is presented." The success of the complex and the survival of jobs depended on it. All enquiries were welcome.

Posters and booklets and leaflets and booking forms had to be prepared. Information about dates, times and ticket prices for as many as nine different attractions a day, over the entire three months of the premiere season, had to be compiled, published and distributed internationally. "Accuracy, accuracy — and facts — no superlatives," was the caution. "We have not heard her sing yet." But accuracy was not so easy when you were coping with all those foreign names. "How do you spell it?" someone almost wept when talking to Japan about the names of the first violins in the Nippon Hoso Kyokai Symphony Orchestra.

Time was running out. Tempers were frayed. Interdepartmental feuds developed. The house services department plainly regarded the publicity department as a lunatic asylum. The publicity department complained that security staff were behaving like prison warders. The theatre lettings department was considered "mischievous". How else could you explain all those bookings for charity ladies' musicales and bodgie pantos?

Helen Reddy, now an American citizen, is still proud to appear in the land of her birth.

Right. In this scene from War and Peace, Napoleon, played by Raymond Myers, sits on a camp chair and makes battle plans.

Petula Clark has always had a large following in Australia and her Opera House appearance was greeted enthusiastically.

Tour guides, publicists and just about everyone else were being warned off by the technical director: "ONCE AND FOR ALL, KEEP OFF THE STAGE! Who are you? Rubbish! You have no business on a stage". He would threaten to throw you off next time.

"No private tours. Strictly forbidden to take parties of friends on a tour of the building," was the command from the executive suite. "I do not care who your mother danced with. No! Not even in your lunch hour. YOU DO NOT HAVE TIME FOR A LUNCH HOUR".

But there was also great dedication. Staff often worked 15 hours a day for two or three weeks on end to get the air-conditioning operating, the publicity material out, and the lavatories flushing. The box office really did not know what a lunch hour meant. Pandemonium!

Enquiries were coming in from all over the world. There were not enough staff. Telephones kept ringing. Someone disconnected the intercom. You walked half a mile if you wanted to speak with the box office manager — and you needed to be a mountaineer — you had to climb over sacks of mail to get into his office.

The box office was a major problem. During the months leading up to the first season, staff complained that they were severely handicapped by inadequate equipment and cramped accommodation. The box office has since been extensively re-designed. Lack of experienced staff was another handicap.

The worldwide publicity generated by the Opera House inspired interstate rivalry and prompted other Australian State Governments to start planning and building performing arts centres in their own capital cities. Nonetheless before the opening of the completed Opera House in September, 1973, there were no major performing arts centres operating at maximum capacity in Australia and few people available with experience in a large theatre complex.

Some box office staff had overseas experience and others had worked in Australian theatre. It was one thing, however, to have experience in a local cinema, or in a theatre with one show on the bill, but quite another to be selling tickets at the new Opera House for as many as nine different events a day, in a variety of theatres, halls and foyers. Just keeping track of the price of tickets was testing under the prevailing conditions. The opening season had almost begun before the racks of pigeon-holes for storing tickets had been installed. Earlier, staff had to make do with shoe-boxes and cartons. No wonder there were continual treasure hunts for mislaid cheques, or missing tickets, worth thousands of dollars.

There was more to do, too, than deal with the thousands of mail orders and over-the-counter sales for current shows. You had to keep thinking ahead, otherwise you might forget to order the printing of tickets for the dozens of forthcoming attractions. But telephone calls

The Opera House can boast symphony concerts graced by the world's most distinguished artists. Among them has been Claudio Arrau, the Chilean pianist, one of a procession of virtuosi.

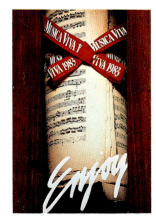

Enjoyment is a key word for the Opera House complex of performing arts, and Musica Viva whose poster this is, has brought infinite pleasure to many thousands of lovers of chamber music.

were the major problem — in the box office — and all other departments. Section heads complained that the non-stop enquiries made it impossible to train new staff, attend to paperwork and otherwise prepare the Opera House for the opening season.

Right. The box office serves the needs of the whole complex. There is always someone enquiring for tickets, or even groups of students waiting for a plan to open.

Don Burrows has established himself as Australia's master of jazz, and holds an academic position in 'teaching' it to serious musicians. He has participated in symphonic concerts when his jazz trio has been the composite soloist.

The Daly Wilson Big Band gave its first Opera House concert on March 14, 1974 and has since given more than 20 Concert Hall performances.

Today the box office accepts telephone bookings seven days a week, and an "Instant Charge" service, which enables patrons to charge telephone orders to their credit card and pick up their tickets immediately prior to the performance, is very popular.

Although the Opera House did not begin to accept telephone orders until 1977, the original team of 15 box office staff did have to answer telephone enquiries about the price of tickets, the availability of seats and the location of seats.

Calls banked up. It was maddeningly time-consuming and frustrating. Patrons complained that they had spent days trying to get through to the box office. They wanted information and patient service, but often got short shrift. Hold-ups occurred because people wanted so much information — and reassurance. Many appeared amazed that the Opera House, nearly 20 years in the planning, was actually open for business. Patrons were confused by the number of theatres and foyers. They wanted a guided tour by phone. They did not have time to search for the advertisement they had lost, or to wait for the arrival of a brochure in the mail. They were anxious to apply for seats immediately — for at least one historic first performance. But which performance?

Many were bewildered by the number and variety of Opera House attractions. They asked for synopses of operas and plays.

The great Swedish soprano, Birgit Nilsson, was the soloist at the first performance in the Concert Hall — an all-Wagner programme, which also featured the Sydney Symphony Orchestra, conducted by Sir Charles Mackerras. "Who is this lass Bridget Nilsson?" someone asked. "Is she any good?" "Is Joan Sutherland in it?" was a frequent query.

Some patrons were nostalgic. They delayed young box office assistants with tales of the old Sydney theatres — The Criterion, Her Majesty's, The Royal, The Gaiety and The Grand Opera House in York Street — theatres that had long since been demolished to make way for new office blocks and stores. People reminisced about queueing in Sydney in the 1920's and 1930's to see Pavlova, Chaliapin and Melba. "I spent nearly a whole week's wages to see Melba," said a man just turning seventy. The Australian soprano, Joan Hammond, was often mentioned, and the musical comedy star of the 1920's, 1930's and 1940's, Gladys Moncrieff. "When are you putting her on?" people wanted to know.

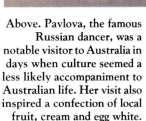

Above. Pavlova, the famous Russian dancer, was a notable visitor to Australia in days when culture seemed a less likely accompaniment to Australian life. Her visit also inspired a confection of local fruit, cream and egg white.

Centre, Gladys Moncrieff, 'Our Glad' to another generation, filled the theatres of Australia with mellifluous song. Her role as The Maid of the Mountains was almost a lifetime encore. Left, Dame Nellie Melba, seen here while still young and long before the frequent farewell concerts which caused so much satirical comment. Her overseas triumphs set an example to many subsequent singers. Above, Dame Joan Hammond, another success story on the European opera stage who returned to a life of operatic teaching in Victoria and whose voice still echoes in dramatic memories.

Gladys Moncrieff, eighty-one, when the Opera House opened in 1973, had been persuaded to travel from her retirement home on the Queensland Gold Coast to open the first show in the Exhibition Hall — an exhibition of Australian and British theatre memorabilia, mounted by the Sydney Opera House Trust and the British Council. This news was greeted with immense delight by many of the over-fifties. It was obvious that few stars of Australian theatre were regarded with as much affection as "our Glad".

With the opening season imminent, the media and the public

wanted to know if Utzon had been invited to the official opening of the Opera House by Queen Elizabeth. Utzon declined his invitation from the New South Wales Government. Years later, in 1978, in an interview for the Sydney Opera House Monthly Diary, he said:

'I would like to explain why I declined the invitation to the official opening. It was not for any negative reasons. I have never had any negative feelings about the Opera House. I thought it was the most diplomatic thing I could to. An enormous number of newspaper people were pursuing me at the time, asking about the 'true story' of the Opera House and my 'bitter recriminations'. I did not want to be involved, at the time, in endless discussions about the past, and I knew there would be no way of avoiding the press if I came to Sydney. I thought my presence at the opening ceremony, especially in the company of people like Davis Hughes, who I knew would be attending, would increase the possibility of the resurrection of controversial issues.

"Publicity of that kind might have overshadowed the celebrations and embarrassed guests who were not involved in those issues. I did what I could to prevent that happening". During that interview, which was conducted by telephone, Utzon was asked: "When you learnt that four Australian architects had agreed to take over from you and complete the Opera House, did you feel betrayed by them? Did you think it was a dishonourable thing for fellow architects to do?" He replied: "You know, I am a fatalist. I do not think it serves any purpose to be negative. When I left Sydney and returned to Denmark my dentist was very anxious to see how much I had been grinding my teeth. He found them in good shape".

When Utzon made these comments he had just received Queen Elizabeth's gold medal for architecture for his design of the Opera House. In a 1978 speech in London to members of the Royal British Institute of Architects, who recommended the award, Utzon said that receipt of the gold medal had helped to heal "any tiny scars" that remained as a legacy of the Opera House project.

Earlier, the Danish civil engineer, Ove Arup, who worked as Utzon's associate, and later as the associate of the four Australian architects who replaced him at the Opera House, had been awarded the British architects' gold medal. Utzon was reported to have been deeply wounded by the news that Arup, the engineer, and not himself, had been the first to be honoured by his British colleagues.

Some experts, however, maintain that the construction of Utzon's Opera House — the fact that his awe-inspiring design was actually realized, despite the seemingly insurmountable engineering problems presented — is the peerless achievement of 20th century construction, and that the engineer, Ove Arup, is the actual unsung hero of the Opera House.

Feodor Chaliapin, the Russian basso, was a huge man whose acting was as impressive as his singing. His Australian tour made him a household name.

Ove Arup, whose engineering genius superbly complemented the aesthetic vision of Jorn Utzon.

In 1966, when preparing to leave Australia, Utzon was quoted as saying "I do not care if they pull the Opera House down", and he dismissed the affair as "malice in blunderland". So even though he was chivalrous in 1978 about his reasons for declining his invitation to the official opening, and even though he seemed pleased by the subsequent success of the Opera House — "people, people everywhere — marvellous!" — it is easy to imagine how dejected he must have felt in 1973, when the imminent opening of the building was attracting worldwide publicity.

Royalty, socialites, politicians, tourists and the media were converging on Sydney. Gala performances, pre-theatre dinners, after-show receptions, glamour gowns and star artists were in the news. Yet the man who created the building would not be there! The heartrending finales of opera pale by comparison.

Claudio Alcorso, a former chairman of The Australian Opera, was a constant stimulus to the company in its formative years. Charles Berg is the present incumbent.

At the time, when Utzon was avoiding the press, his gallant reasons for refusing his invitation to the official opening were not widely known in Australia. It was assumed he was merely "bitter". To add insult to injury he was accused of "sour grapes" and of "snubbing the Queen". He was reported to be in hiding in Hawaii. In fact, he was fulfilling lecturing engagements at the University of Hawaii.

Meanwhile, the Royal Australian Institute of Architects made its position plain. Just before Queen Elizabeth opened the Opera House, members of the institute awarded Utzon their own gold medal. The medal was mailed to Utzon as he had declined to receive the award personally in Sydney.

Utzon has received other awards for his design of the Opera House. These include the Alva Aalto Medal, awarded by Finnish architects in 1982 for "the use of unique and innovative forms, many of which are without precedent in the history of architecture". When interviewed in 1978, Utzon appeared cheerful and as fatalistic as he had claimed. "I never comment on a lobster until I have eaten it," he said when asked his opinion of photographs of the interior of the Opera House designed by Peter Hall.

The open areas around the halls are often filled with people and even latecomers can view the performance on television monitors.

In a 1980 interview for the Opera House Diary, however, he proved more emotional. During that interview he was asked to comment on a suggestion, made by a former chairman of The Australian Opera, Claudio Alcorso, that the Opera House be enlarged. Alcorso claimed that an extra theatre, suitable for grand opera and an audience of 3,000, could be built on the eastern side of the Opera House, over Sydney Harbour. "I wonder how he would feel," Utzon asked, "if I suggested that a new movement be added to Beethoven's first symphony, or a new act, written in our time, be added to Aida?"

During that interview, Utzon became particularly upset when he spoke of the interiors he had designed for the Opera House, "as com-

Left. Like some great Leviathan, the Opera House can be circumnavigated, climbed over, explored, and the promenade and stairways are nearly always swarming with eager people.

missioned", and a major theatre that was to have featured partitions and stage machinery that would have made it suitable for performances ranging from grand opera to chamber music. He sounded irritated on the phone by the idea of people imagining that he is responsible for the interior design as it now stands. "Where are my plans?" he demanded. "They must be somewhere in Sydney. They should be on public view."

These comments suggest his changing states of mind about the Opera House, and the anguish he must have suffered over the project; but in a letter, written in 1981, he recalls his joy in 1957 when his daughter, Lin, then ten years of age, received the telephone call bringing "the fabulous news" that he had won the Opera House contest. He was out walking in the forest. She chased him on her bicycle, threw it in a ditch and told him he would be able to buy her a white horse.

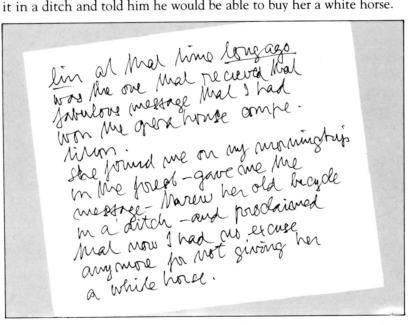

Part of an actual letter written to the author by Utzon, recalling the excitement his success in the Opera House design competition brought to his family.

When interviewed in 1978 and 1980 he retained icy control when mentioning Davis Hughes. Yet his warmth was tangible when he asked for his greetings to be passed on to the men who had supported him. "I have never had any negative feelings about the Opera House", Utzon claimed in an interview, but in a letter later he confides "to be honest, I do not like the interiors and I am sure I would like them even less if I saw them in Sydney".

He has said he was never reduced to grinding his teeth, but he fought back his fury when he spoke of stage machinery he ordered for the major theatre being "torn down", and when it was suggested that his Opera House be enlarged, he was very much the protective artist, understandably aghast at the idea of any more tinkering with his much publicised building.

Sir Charles Moses has said he thinks that Sydney people would now like the opportunity of cheering Utzon in the streets. When she visited Sydney in 1980-81, the architect's daughter, Lin Utzon, said she would like her father to sail around the Opera House, but that she would not like him to see "what has been done inside". She also said she would be apprehensive about the reaction of the media if her father returned. "Someday, perhaps . . ." Utzon has said about another visit to Sydney.

The formation of government funded opera, ballet and drama companies began in Australia in 1956. Earlier, in 1932, the first government funded orchestras were established by the Australian Broadcasting Commission. Prior to 1932 all performances in Australia were presented by independent entrepreneurs, principally J. C. Williamson's — "The Firm" — which has been in business in Australia and New Zealand for about a hundred years, since 1874.

Arthur Rubinstein, who died in 1983, seemed indestructible and his pianistic prowess touched even the Antipodes.

In the early decades of this century independent impresarios occasionally arranged for leading European opera and ballet companies to tour Australia and in 1934 the Australian Broadcasting Commission began importing celebrated conductors and soloists to appear with its concert ensembles. The great pianists Arthur Schnabel and Arthur Rubinstein, the soprano Toti Dal Monte, the legendary ballerina Anna Pavlova, conductor Malcolm Sargent and stars of the De Basil Ballet Russe de Monte Carlo were among the artists who said they enjoyed the long, leisurely sea voyage out to Australia, the chance to tour the vast continent and bask for a few months in the warmth of the Australian sunshine.

Australian audiences, cut off by time and distance from the great performing capitals of the world, with no great companies of their own, and no radio or television to keep them at home, would queue for hours to buy tickets for the performances of visiting artists, and huge crowds would gather at quaysides and railway stations to welcome the stars. Sarah Bernhardt was treated like royalty.

Arthur Schnabel, one of the most memorable interpreters of Beethoven's piano sonatas, was a virtuoso who received ovations in Australia.

Before World War II Australian audiences regarded performances, especially of opera and ballet, as great and rare occasions demanding full evening dress. Some local cartoonists have not caught up with the changing times. They persist in portraying the typical operagoer in boiled shirt and tail coat, or as an extravagantly draped dowager. But today, dressing for Opera House performances is decidedly mixed. Lounge suits and simple dresses, as well as dinner jackets and glamorous evening gowns, are worn to opera and ballet premieres. Dressing for plays and concerts is generally even more varied. Jeans are often sported — shorts less frequently — although a young couple were photographed arriving for the 1981 Opera House premiere of Verdi's Otello in shorts, with knapsacks on their backs. They were only asked to cloak their bulging knapsacks.

Edouard Borovansky, the inspiration of the ballet in Australia, and a reminder of the debt owed to many migrants to this continent.

Left. Joan Sutherland as Desdemona and Angelo Marenzi as Otello in the dramatic opera based on Shakespeare's immortal tragedy of the Moor.

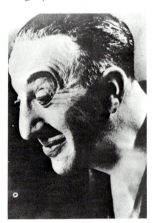

Roy Rene, or 'Mo' of vaudeville fame, whom Australian comics still revere as the master.

The management certainly does not impose restrictions about dress — it even encourages the musicians, as well as the audience, to wear tee-shirts and jeans for the annual Mostly Mozart series.

World War II and its recriminating aftermath put a stop to the Australian tours of celebrated European companies and artists.

Following the war, the old Sydney theatres which had not been torn down to make way for new development, were converted into cinemas, or were used for the most popular live entertainments of the day — musical comedy and vaudeville. By the mid-1940's there was certainly no opera theatre worthy of the name in Sydney.

At the time, there were conservatoriums and a few privately-run academies in Australia, where singers, musicians, dancers and actors could study. But there were few opportunities in those days, and for some years after, for Australian artists to work regularly at home. Australians were in the casts of the musicals, plays and vaudeville shows presented, but often merely as chorus members, or as artists supporting imported English and American stars.

Gladys Moncrieff and the comedian, Roy Rene, were certainly adored by pre-war audiences. But they were among the few Australians who became stage stars in their own country without first proving themselves overseas.

Until the opening of the Opera House and the new theatre complexes subsequently built in other cities, Australian artists were not taken seriously at home unless they had studied and worked successfully overseas — when they returned home in triumph — as Nellie Melba did in 1902, and Joan Sutherland did in 1965 — as visiting expatriates with international reputations as superstars.

Clarice Lorenz, by the Australian artist. Hayward Veal.

But not everyone living in Australia in the 1930's and 1940's lacked confidence in local talent. There was a handful of people with great dreams of national opera and ballet companies, symphony orchestras in every state, and regular orchestral series for school children.

This inspired group included the Australian conductors Bernard Heinze and Joseph Post, the choreographer and ballet dancer, Edouard Borovansky, the general manager of the Australian Broadcasting Commission, Sir Charles Moses, the theatre lover, Gertrude Johnson, and the music lover and society hostess, Clarice Lorenz — who was often accused of sending her husband, a leading optician, and her friends almost bankrupt in her efforts to form a national opera company and create more work for Australian orchestral players.

But these people were primarily interested in forming orchestras and companies. The man responsible for suggesting a magnificent home for those orchestras and companies was, of course, Sir Eugene Goossens. Goossens is now also credited with prompting the great Australia-wide explosion of interest in new theatre complexes and the performing arts which followed in the wake of the decision to build the Opera House.

A portrait of the Australian conductor, Sir Bernard Heinze by the Viennese-born artist, Louis Kahan.

CURTAIN CALL

Life at the Opera House begins

Captain James Cook, navigator of the eastern coast of Australia viewed Sydney Harbour from its ocean entrance but did not sail into its placid waters. Nonetheless, his discovery of Botany Bay and Port Jackson led to the final settlement in 1788.

Left. Twilight brings an increasing tempo of activity to the theatres on Bennelong Point, as lights shine from windows and promenade.

O ne of the heroes of English naval history, the explorer Captain James Cook, mapped the east coast of Australia in 1770, during the first of his three great voyages of discovery. The continent was colonized for the first time for the British in 1788, when Captain Arthur Phillip sailed into Sydney Harbour as commander of the first fleet and first governor of New South Wales.

Captain Phillip was originally "bound for Botany Bay", about ten nautical miles to the south, but after finding the recommended "fine meadows" of the bay "a perfect quagmire" — no place to found an infant settlement — and affording little shelter for his 11-ship fleet, he sailed on, arriving in Sydney Harbour on what is now Australia Day — January 26, 1788.

"We got to Port Jackson in the early afternoon and had the satisfaction of finding the finest harbour in the world in which a thousand sail of the line may ride in the most perfect security," recorded the enthusiastic Phillip.

The newly arrived administrators and new settlers, who included over 650 convicts, came ashore at Sydney Cove, a short distance from a peninsular jutting into Port Jackson. That point is now the site of the Opera House. In 1788 it was bushland. It was later cleared for grazing and became known as Cattle Point.

In 1789 an Aborigine called Bennelong, then about twenty-five, was taken captive by one of Governor Phillip's officers. Unlike most of his fellow Aborigines, Bennelong proved engaging and amenable and he soon became Governor Phillip's pampered pet.

At Bennelong's request, Governor Phillip built him a brick dwelling, four metres — 12 ft — square on Cattle Point. The peninsular then became known as Bennelong Point.

Initially, Governor Phillip intended to employ Bennelong as a link man between his administration and the resentful Aborigines, but with little success. Bennelong, although he learned to speak English, had little patience for painstaking, day to day diplomacy. Instead, to the

Captain Arthur Phillip was the first governor of the settlement of Sydney Cove and lived above the point on which the Opera House now stands. His treatment of the indigenous people, whom he called 'Indians', was respectful and humane.

Government House, from a watercolour by William Westall, 1781-1850. This building replaced the earlier wattle and daub structure which Bennelong visited, and which stood on the rise just above his dwelling on the point.

A hand-coloured print of Bennelong, about 1804, from an anonymous etching now in the possession of the Opera House Trust.

amusement of the indulgent Phillip, he merely adopted the way of life of an 18th century European idler.

He became a frequent visitor at Government House. There, decked out in the new finery provided by Phillip, he aped the manners of the English officers and developed a taste for brandy and the delicacies served at the governor's table. The increasingly sophisticated Bennelong returned the hospitality in 1791, when it was recorded that he "entertained Governor Phillip and party at his hut on Bennelong Point".

In the following year, 1792, when Phillip retired, he invited Bennelong and another Aborigine, the boy Yemmerrawannie, to accompany him home.

On May 24, 1793, the day after Phillip arrived in England, he introduced both Aborigines to the king, George III.

"The Natives of New South Wales, brought to England by Governor Phillip, were yesterday at a window in St James's Street, to see the company going to St James's. What their ideas were, we will not attempt to guess," reported the patronizing Lloyd's Evening Post.

Both Bennelong and the boy, Yemmerrawannie, suffered terribly in the English climate. Yemmerrawannie did not survive the visit. He sickened and died in London in 1794.

A series of eight oil paintings about the life of Bennelong by the Australian artist, Donald Friend, hangs in the general manager's office at the Opera House. One of the pictures depicts him, his hands clapped to his ears, "suffering Handel" during a drawing-room musicale he is reported to have attended in England.

Right. The Bennelong series of paintings by Donald Friend hang in the General Manager's office. They follow the chequered career of the Aborigine most favoured by Governor Phillip. Bennelong was a frequent guest at Government House. Dressed in European clothes, he tasted European food and was forced to listen to European music the tonality of which hardly pleased him.

Bennelong, however, survived not only the music and the rigours of the English climate, but the long voyage back to Australia. He returned to Sydney with Arthur Phillip's successor, Governor John Hunter in 1795, and took up residence at Government House where, for a time, he is reported to have been regarded as "almost an exhibit".

Bennelong's hut on Bennelong Point was dismantled in 1796, although the reason is not recorded. Nor does any detailed, day to day account of his life exist, but from bits and pieces of recorded biographical information, we know that he had two wives, Banangaroo and Goroobarooboolo, and a son who survived him.

After being taken up by Governor Phillip, however, Bennelong seems to have lost close contact with his family, and when he returned from England with Governor Hunter, he often appeared to be contemptuous of the ways of his own people. Yet he never entirely rejected them — and certainly not the women of his tribe. Bennelong was a womanizer. Following his return to Sydney he also became notorious as a violent drunk. He is said to have spent his later years either hanging around Government House, attacking or attempting to ingratiate himself with successive administrations, or going bush, invariably well stocked up with liquor, to chase women on the outskirts of town.

His behaviour often involved him in tribal skirmishes. His life of comparative luxury and privilege undoubtedly led to jealousy and a sense of betrayal among his own people, although most of his fights were alleged to have been over women.

The final canvas in Donald Friend's portrayal depicts the "Death of Bennelong", in his 18th century finery, from spear wounds. He is reported to have been wounded in a tribal fight at Kissing Point in 1805,

Captain Hunter followed in the same traditions as those set by his predecessor, Governor Phillip, and became the infant colony's ruler in 1795.

Governor Lachlan Macquarie was not a naval man but commanded an army regiment. He had a great propensity for building and in a scene, below left, from F.C. Terry's An Australian Keepsake, 1855, Sydney Cove is viewed from Fort Macquarie built on Bennelong Point.

These fig trees are more than a century old but if the plan to build a car park beneath the Royal Botanic Gardens had been carried out, the trees would have been removed.

but according to most accounts he died at Parramatta in 1813, mortally debilitated by alcohol, when he would have been about forty-nine years of age. Whatever his end, Bennelong is the first identifiable Aborigine corrupted by white settlers.

A few years after his death, the point with which his name is identified became the site of a fortress, Fort Macquarie, named after the fifth New South Wales Governor, Lachlan Macquarie. The fort, built in 1817, was designed by the renowned convict architect, Francis Greenway (1770-1837).

In 1902 a large tram depot, incorporating the historic fort, was constructed on Bennelong Point. In 1956 this tram depot was converted to a bus station, and three years later, in 1958, the building was razed to make way for the construction of the Opera House.

The Opera House covers 1.82 hectares — 4½ acres — of its 2.23 hectare — 5½ acres — site, which was slightly enlarged to accommodate the building and its surrounding broadwalk.

A car park for the Opera House beneath the adjoining Royal Botanic Gardens had been planned by Utzon and the Australian architects who replaced him.

In 1972, however, when construction was about to begin, it was discovered that the project would entail moving three Moreton Bay Fig Trees (Macrophylla Ficus), which had been standing in the gardens on the foreshores of Sydney Harbour for about 130 years.

As there was doubt whether the historic trees could be successfully replanted, the New South Wales branch of the Builders' Labourers' Federation, then headed by the well-known conservationist and communist, Jack Mundey, refused to co-operate, and work on the proposed car park never began.

Jack Mundey, the Builders' Labourers' Federation and their Green Ban were denounced. In 1972 there was little community support for the conservation of trees. The public's fury intensified when it was announced that no suitable alternative site was available. The Opera House would have no car park.

It was then that the Sydney Opera House Trust announced a Park & Ride bus service for Opera House patrons, an announcement which met with derision. The idea of travelling to the opera by bus outraged the silver-tails, inspired the cartoonists and confirmed the general public in its belief that the Opera House was a disaster area. But the years have seen the service, now advertised as "the next best thing to a chauffeur", accepted and popular. Patrons park in the Domain Parking Station, ten minutes away and are carried by Mercedes buses marked 'Opera House On Charter' to the theatre entrances.

People of all ages, matrons in floor-length gowns, youngsters straight from the beach and bound for a surfing movie in sundresses and shorts, regularly Park & Ride, and anyone who wants candid opinions about Opera House shows need only join the procession as they board the buses after performances.

1982 saw aquacabs introduced by a private operator. These water taxis will pick up from any private or public wharf on Sydney's extensive waterfront from places as far up the Parramatta River as Homebush and Duck Creek, or as near the heads as Watson's Bay or Forty Baskets near Manly. They deliver and pick up patrons at the Opera House wharf — a few metres from the theatre entrances. Glass-encased cabins, which seat up to eight, offer changing scenes of harbour life as they vie for custom against ferry and hydrofoil in all weathers.

Early in 1973 it was announced that the Opera House forecourt would be reserved for pedestrians, but many artists threatened to boycott the complex if they could not park on site during rehearsals and performances. Plans were hastily changed and parking was provided for 400 cars for the disabled, performers, staff, and critics.

Initially, premier Cahill hoped to raise enough money to build the Opera House from public donations. He established the Sydney Opera House Appeal Fund in August, 1957. Business firms, society hostesses,

Aquacabs, carrying up to eight passengers, were laughed at when first suggested but have now become an exciting way of arriving for an Opera House performance.

The failure to provide a car park was long seen as a disadvantage but the Park and Ride Bus Service from the Domain Parking Station has now become one of the novelties of a night at the Opera House, and an established institution.

Right. The Opera House is seen in proper scale from the open forecourt where its huge dimensions are best realised, framed against sea and sky.

and children, who contributed a few pence of their pocket money were among the donors. Their names are listed in a book in the Box Office foyer and a different page is turned each day.

Between August and December, 1957, approximately £450,000 ($900,000) was donated; a commendable effort but as the original estimate for the Opera House was £3½ million ($7 million), it was totally inadequate. As the New South Wales Government had been conducting lotteries to raise revenue for public works since 1932, in 1958 Cahill started yet another — the Opera House Lottery. The first prize would be £100,000 — a spending power of $800,000 in 1983 — and more than enough in 1958 to set you up for the rest of your life. At £3 ($6) each — an apprentice's wage in 1958 — the lottery tickets were considered expensive, but from the very first draw there was a rush to buy, and the lottery has never lost its popularity.

Initially, many happy winners were pictured on the front pages, but later most gamblers signified that their names should not be published, a precaution which followed a tragedy.

In June, 1960, as a result of his father's name being published eight-year-old Graeme Thorne was kidnapped, offered for ransom and murdered. The crime outraged Australia. Even members of the underworld were reported to have offered assistance to police, who apprehended the killer, Stephen Bradley, within weeks.

On July 31, 1975, twenty-two months after the Opera House had opened, the New South Wales Government announced that the final cost of building, equipping and furnishing the complex was $102 million. This had been met from the $900,000 raised by the 1957 appeal fund, and the balance of just over $101 million from lottery profits.

Between the first draw, on January 10, 1958 and July 31, 1975, 496 lotteries were conducted. 100,000 six-dollar tickets were sold in each lottery. A grand total of $297,600,000 was gathered from the sale of the 49,600,000 six-dollar tickets. After a pay-out of $190,196,160 in major and minor prizes, a total gross profit of $107,403,840 was realized. During the sixteen and a half years between January, 1958 and July, 1975, the cost of administering the lottery amounted to approximately $6½ million — so the net profit was about $101 million. Several times during construction lottery profits failed to keep up with building costs and the government had to provide bridging finance.

The Opera House Lottery is still being regularly conducted, but since 1975 profits have been paid into consolidated revenue. The New South Wales Government, however, has provided about 40% of the annual running costs since the building opened in 1973. It currently costs about $20 million a year to maintain and operate the complex and mount productions, but as Australia's premiere tourist attraction, and the country's leading performing arts centre, the building now helps to

Mr Sellers was the first winner of an Opera House Lottery in January, 1958. The first prize brought joy as well as sorrow to a great series of winners.

No Opera House performance could be mounted without the varied backstage operations. Less glamorous in style, these are the nuts and bolts of theatrical production and occupy long hours and heavy labour.

The Australian Opera chorus rehearses on stage for its role in La Boheme while determined planning goes on around them.

earn more than $1,000 million a year in tourist revenue from overseas.

No wonder the Opera House, once so frequently condemned as an unnecessary extravagance, is now regarded as one of the best real estate investments ever made!

The complex is one of the world's busiest, open for 15 hours a day every day of the year except Christmas Day and Good Friday. An average of nine events a day is presented. Many comparable centres and opera houses in other countries — La Scala, Milan — for example, are closed for several weeks each year.

Backstage at the Opera House rehearsals are conducted night and day, and staff are at work preparing the building for performances and rehearsals 24 hours a day throughout the year.

The promenade surrounding the building, like the top deck of a luxury liner, is always open to strollers.

"You actually get paid for working here?" visitors often ask when they see the panorama and parade from the windows of Opera House offices. There are "million dollar views" of great stretches of Sydney Harbour. The Queen Elizabeth II, the Canberra and other cruise ships

glide majestically by, their passengers lining the decks, waving a greeting to promenaders and staff at the Opera House windows. There is a continous traffic of gigantic container ships, oil tankers, naval vessels, ferries and yachts and the fast-moving hydrofoils and aquacabs often appear to be on a collision course with the Opera House, but then miraculously wheel, seemingly centimetres from the promenade, and dash onwards to berth safely at Circular Quay.

That the Opera House has become a tourist mecca is evident when you stroll around the promenade. You see as many nationalities and hear as many foreign languages as at an international airport. To guarantee a seat at the Opera House overseas visitors book package tours through the Opera House's tourism and marketing division. The most popular package, called "An Evening at the Sydney Opera" can be booked up to a year ahead. It features an early evening tour, followed by dinner at the main restaurant, the Bennelong, and a performance. A typical pre-theatre dinner menu offers seasonal fruit platter, sea perch

The Opera House is surrounded by water on three sides and sea-going vessels of every size pass its static white sails bound for the ocean. Here the cruise ship, S.S. Canberra prepares to berth at the Overseas Shipping Terminal in Sydney Cove.

Right. The Bennelong Restaurant is set below the smallest of the Opera House sails. It serves luncheons, dinners and suppers but its most frequent patrons are guaranteed completion of their meal in time for that evening's performance.

Outdoor concerts vary from the serious to the light-hearted. Here the famous singing trio, Peter, Paul and Mary, entertain a vast audience.

souffle with mousseline sauce, or soup of the day; braised silverside of beef, breast of chicken marenchale with asparagus in brown butter, or fisherman's catch of the day, and coffee and mints.

Guided tours began on a daily basis in July, 1973 — a couple of months before the premiere season. Very soon tour guides began to complain that Opera House publicists ignored how taxing it could be escorting parties of forty or fifty inquisitive members of the general public around the Opera House, yet such publicists were only too ready to relieve guides if film stars, sporting identities and other celebrities were to be shown over the building. One guide even had ambitions to marry Glenn Ford, and had been assured she would be his escort on his Opera House tour only to discover that she had been replaced by a public relations assistant! Then the management intervened: all tours, even those for visiting royalty, prime ministers, presidents and celebrities, would be led by staff guides. Publicists could meet, interview and photograph celebrities after their tour. Harmony was restored.

The Opera House has the reputation of being the scene of more "first performances" than any other theatre in history. During the fourteen years the complex was under construction, hundreds of stars, including Johnny Ray, Paul Robeson, Louis Armstrong, Margot Fonteyn and Peter, Paul and Mary, were invited to don safety helmets and tour the building site. At the request of the media, some of the stars gave a performance for construction workers. They would sing a few bars, dance a few steps, or, like Peter, Paul and Mary, present a carefully stage-managed lunchtime concert for workers, filmed for television news. Such events were invariably described incorrectly as the "first performance at the Opera House" and successive test programmes were often similarly billed.

Nearly 200,000 people a year go on guided tours of the complex. They are mostly overseas, country or inter-state visitors, or school-children.

In fact the first major acoustics test was presented in the Concert Hall, on the afternoon of Sunday, December 17, 1972. At that time, the complex was still under construction, its forecourt and surrounding broadwalk unpaved and lifts and other facilities not yet running. But most people were too excited to worry about the inconvenience. Acoustics test it may officially have been, but as far as the audience was concerned, the concert was the "first performance at the Opera House" The Sydney Symphony Orchestra was conducted by Sir Bernard Heinze. In the invited audience were construction workers and their families, Sir Robert Askin, the premier of the day, the chief justice of New South Wales, Sir John Kerr — later to become Australia's most controversial governor-general — and Sydney's leading music critics.

Neville Marriner, then conductor of the Academy of St. Martin-in-the-Fields, found the acoustics flattering to his ensemble.

Opera House publicists tried in vain to dissuade the critics from reviewing the test concert. At the time the publicity department was working to ensure worldwide coverage for the opening season. They wanted no scoops, no previews, no final verdicts on the Opera House as a performing arts centre until that season began. They feared that reviews of test events would confuse the public and the overseas media and upstage the premiere performances. The task of ridding the Opera House of its white elephant image was difficult enough without having the acoustics damned before the complex was even officially opened. But the acoustics test was a success. It produced the first positive reports about the complex in years. Under the headline "Concert Hall looks good and sounds even better" the Sydney Morning Herald's reviewer, Professor Roger Covell, wrote on December 18, 1972:

Roger Covell, Music Critic of the Sydney Morning Herald.

"No final pronouncements can be made yet, of course. But a first hearing of the Sydney Symphony Orchestra in the concert hall of the Sydney Opera House at yesterday afternoon's test performance was distinctly encouraging . . .

"We may have a first-class concert hall, or something very close to it on our hands . . .

"It is already clear that the orchestral masterworks and showpieces of, say, Ravel, Debussy, Stravinsky will be effective as never before in this city. The exciting performances of Ravel's 'Bolero' given under Sir Bernard Heinze's direction made that as certain as anything can be at this stage."

Sir Bernard was quoted as saying "I found the hall delightful in its resonance and its ability to reproduce the individual sounds of the various instruments in their own particular colours. From a conductor's point of view, that is what I want".

The Concert Hall's acoustics have been praised ever since. "Second to none," was the verdict of Joan Sutherland. "Better than honest — flattering," said Neville Marriner. "There is a feeling of intimacy and the sound carries easily," said Claudio Arrau. "Good," said Leonard Bernstein. "Marvellous," was the opinion of the Australian guitarist, John Williams. "No one with ears could complain about the acoustics in the Concert Hall," said the conductor, Walter Susskind. As for the acoustics of the Opera Theatre they are said to flatter singers. "It is like singing in my bathroom," announced the American soprano, Leona Mitchell.

Rock concerts were eventually consigned to external performance on the Opera House forecourt. The use of the Concert Hall saw enthusiasm and physical participation lead to damage to seating and fabric.

Leonard Bernstein brought the New York Philharmonic Orchestra to Australia in 1974. He showed himself sensitive to the enthusiasm of music-lovers, especially those unable to attend the scheduled concerts.

Dr Wilhelm Lassen Jordan proved a remarkable acoustics engineer, and produced a viable system capable of adjustment to music groups of differing size and gave general satisfaction with the acoustics of the Opera House theatres and halls.

All Opera House theatres are used for a much wider range of events than originally envisaged, and work goes ahead to improve the acoustics for various types of entertainment from rock to opera. Therefore the search continues for the ideal amplification system for the Concert Hall where there have been sound distortion problems during rock and variety shows. Another problem is the difficulty of hearing every unamplified word of spoken dialogue from some seats in the Concert Hall and the Opera Theatre. Among the many measures recommended to correct these defects are the use of lead vinyl for set draperies, instead of softer fabrics which absorb sound; hard, reflecting materials, such as plywood for sets, and hard paint for scenery. Even so, the acoustics are generally regarded as one of the Opera House's strongest points. They were designed by the Danish acoustics scientist, Wilhelm Lassen Jordan. Dr Jordan became a member of Jorn Utzon's design team in 1957. He remained the Opera House's acoustics consultant until his death, during a working visit to Sydney in 1982. His son and associate, Nils Jordan, has replaced him as the management's acoustics adviser.

In spite of the controversial conversion of the intended opera theatre to a concert hall, superb performances of both opera and ballet have been staged there. Left. The classical tour de force of Swan Lake sweeps across the stage. Below left. Beethoven's only opera, Fidelio, rises to its dramatic heights with John Shaw as Don Fernando. Below. Glenys Fowles and Anson Austin play the roles of Romeo and Juliette in Gounod's opera of the Shakespeare play.

Shortly before the Opera House opened in 1973, it was announced that test events had shown that opera, ballet and other stage shows could be presented in the Concert Hall. Following the controversy provoked by the 1967 decision to convert the major multi-purpose theatre into the Concert Hall, it was expected that this news would enrage the public. After all there was no stage machinery, orchestral pit or adequate wing space But the expected outcry never occurred. By then most people, and even the media, had given up attempting to account for the ever-changing decisions at Bennelong Point, and had decided to wait and judge for themselves.

The Concert Hall is now successfully used for many purposes despite its lack of a proscenium arch and stage curtains. The great ingenuity of producers, designers and lighting masters has led to the presentation of Verdi's Aida and Nabucco, Strauss's Salome, Tchaikovsky's Swan Lake, Gounod's Romeo and Juliette, and many variety spectaculars.

Sir Robert Helpmann, the apparently indestructible dancer, choreographer, actor, director, all of whose skills have been displayed at the Opera House. He is pictured here in a famous role, Don Quixote.

Although the acoustic tests were successful, some of the other test events, held in the months leading up to the premiere season were disasters. There was the night of the multi-test performances in April, 1972, when four theatres were put to use simultaneously for the first time. Front-of-house staff were told that the first rule of good theatre management is to ensure that the audience is seated on time. But with curtain-time imminent, inexperienced staff and confused patrons chased each other around the complex in an increasingly frenzied war dance as they attempted to locate theatre seats that matched the brandished tickets.

Rudolf Nureyev, with a world reputation as a dancer and choreographer, has been guest artist with the Australian Ballet on a number of occasions.

Perhaps the most disastrous event in the Opera House's history was the "gala" held on July 19, 1973. The event was organized by Lady Mary Fairfax to raise money for The Australian Ballet. The public was invited to pay $50 — the equivalent of $140 today — to see a preview screening of Don Quixote, starring Rudolph Nureyev, Lucette Aldous and Robert Helpmann, followed by a champagne supper with the official party, which included the Governor of New South Wales, Sir Roden Cutler and Lady Cutler. The preview attracted front page publicity and was quickly sold out. Like so many test events, it was touted as "the first performance at the Opera House".

The publicity department was furious with the management for permitting the affair. The headlines about $50 tickets convinced many people that the Opera House would cater only for the wealthy and added to the international confusion about the exact opening date.

The stage was set for a fiasco which might have been scripted by the Marx Brothers when, in the gloom of a winter's evening, nearly 3,000 gala goers were seen groping their way through the obstacle course of the construction site.

Women clutched their escorts as they wove their way around workmen's sheds and over the still unpaved ground. High heels snapped, evening clothes were besmirched. Massed bands on the monumental steps played stoically to herald the arrival of the paying guests. Few were cheered by the music. Several women wanted to go home when they reached the cloakrooms and saw that their hair-styles had been ruined by the dank night air.

In the crush, waiters with trays held aloft on one palm, imperiously attempted balletic twirls on the spot, spilling as much champagne as they served. But the high point of the black comedy came when it was realized that staff and bandsmen had devoured most of the banquet prepared for the guests!

If that night was a debacle, the final months leading up to the premiere season were a nightmare.

Two months before, when it had been announced with fanfare that The Australian Opera would present Prokofiev's epic War and Peace as the first performance, the composer Larry Sitsky held a news conference on the steps of the Opera House to announce that his one-act opera, The Fall of the House of Usher, never performed before or since, would, in fact, be the first opera to be presented. "But only as a test performance," he was reminded. "You can only open a can of sardines once," retorted Sitsky. He was quoted around the world. It was during the test performances of a double bill of Australian operas — Sitsky's "Usher", and "Dalgerie" by James Penberthy in July, 1973, that it was discovered that 98 box seats in the Opera Theatre had no view (or an extremely restricted one) of the stage.

James Penberthy's one-act opera, Dalgerie, made up one half of the double bill at the first 'test night' in the Opera Theatre. It was then discovered that nearly 100 seats had a defective view of the stage.

Larry Sitsky, whose opera, The Fall of the House of Usher was presented during test performances in July 1973. The composer insisted that it was the first opera to be premiered at the Opera House.

Left. A scene from War and Peace, the Prokofiev opera based on Tolstoy's epic work set during Napoleon's invasion of Czarist Russia.

For several weeks prior to the first official performances, the Opera House was in the confusing state of being half open. Guided tours were being conducted, conventions catered for, the box office was in operation, the main restaurant and the self-service restaurant on the promenade were in service. Companies were moving in for rehearsals. Yet right up until the day of the premiere of War and Peace, workmen were racing to complete interior decorations and installations, and many areas of the complex remained out of bounds.

Had it not been for the presence of Queen Elizabeth and the Duke of Edinburgh, the premiere season may very well have been presented as something of an aftermath.

There were newspaper stories about a "police state at Bennelong Point," and complaints about "locks, bolts, chains, scowls and lists of things verboten".

Right. The Opera House not only took much longer to build than was originally expected, 1959 to 1973, but its cost also rose astronomically.

Builders, carpenters, painters, plumbers and electricians would have liked the opportunity of completing their work before even staff, let alone rehearsing artists and patrons moved in.

Some of the construction workers seemed to resent the newcomers bitterly. After 14 years of having the Opera House as an island all to themselves, they were reluctant to hand over to a new regime.

Their resentment often manifested itself in harsh commands to the Opera House staff to get out even though they were attempting to master the geography of the complex — conducting tours, or pointing out facilities to entrepreneurs. Foremen even complained that women guides, publicists, usherettes and stenographers were distracting their men, and causing hold-ups while the men themselves often made highly offensive remarks about staff passing by.

Pamela Stephenson as Polly Peachum on The Old Tote's opening season production of The Threepenny Opera.

Left. The Threepenny Opera, by Bertold Brecht, seemed to some playgoers a daring innovation. Brecht's radical use of theatre was largely unknown until the Old Tote presented this famous work.

It was riveting theatre but nobody seemed inspired to jot down the dialogue for future use in operas or plays and as the management was primarily concerned with the completion of the Opera House and the prevention of a last minute strike on the site, staff were told simply to make the best of it.

The first performers to move into the Opera House for daily rehearsals were members of The Australian Opera. Here was another rude awakening for stage-struck staff. Performers could be even more demanding and critical than public and press. Artists proved pleasant enough when approached for autographs or publicity pictures, but they needed time to settle in and they became impatient when tracking down rehearsal studios and dressing rooms. They said they would never find their way to the stage. Egos were bruised at the stage door when people were challenged about their identity. Everyone seemed to expect security staff to know their names and faces.

There were other difficulties: experiments with the two stage revolves in the Opera Theatre threatened to scalp the musicians in the orchestral pit below and the pit was denounced as ridiculously small. Inadequate wing space was another cause of criticism. The 60-strong chorus for the performance of War and Peace was lined up for rehearsals in a crocodile that stretched from the wings, down a passageway and flight of stairs into the Green Room.

The Old Tote Theatre Company also moved in only to find the Drama Theatre's access for scenery was so limited that large sets had to be cut up, carried in sections, and built-up again on the stage.

The staff usually suffered the brunt of the dissatisfaction and teething pains though in no way responsible for the design or equipment. They soon realized their role would be that of the factotum and it was discovered that stars prefer the company of other stars. They are primarily concerned with their next performance and preparations for that performance. They do not want to be distracted or waylaid by small talk. Congratulations are acceptable after performance, but woe betide an usher, or even a theatre manager, who dares to call at the star's dressingroom for a chat before performance or rehearsal. "We are working," objected a rehearsing prima donna when an official attempted to introduce her to a former British prime minister and his wife during a guided tour.

"Only the most successful artists can fill the large halls," said an executive from Carnegie Hall. "The others go from the small halls, to school halls to church halls, to the graveyard." Yet when you stand in the wings, watching the big theatres fill up with expectant patrons, noticing the critics arriving, you often think that the graveyard would be a better alternative. You wonder why anyone would actually want to go out and face the music; how artists summon up the courage even to walk out onto the stage. As you watch even the most eminent artists, apprehensively awaiting their cue, you realize what agony stage fright must be, and you understand why they have so little time for small talk and other people's affairs. Every performance is a new trial, with every lapse noted. The critics are only too ready to pounce and savage. Two or three bad reviews can threaten a career. Failures are not tolerated. Backstage assistants are as disappointed as paying customers by poor performances. Unsuccessful, uninspiring artists are left to get home the best way they can. The triumphant stars and new discoveries are spirited away by the rich and influential to celebration parties. Staff remain to clear and prepare for a new day. The theatre is a tough world; but it is a constantly exciting and challenging world.

Despite threats that they would resign as soon as the opening season got under way, most of the original team of the Opera House remains. If there are still arguments and questions backstage, there is also great camaraderie and a sense of accomplishment. The white elephant has become one of the world's most celebrated performing arts centres.

Performers tend to dominate any performing arts complex but designers play a crucial role. Here Wendy Dickson's colourful sketch of a street-singer in The Threepenny Opera makes the point.

Melanie's Australian tour in 1977 was presented by Australian Concert Entertainment. She appeared at the Opera House with Emile Pandolfi (piano), Allen Bondar (electric keyboard), Dave Doran (guitar), Jay Wolfe (bass guitar) and Robert Wise (drums).

GRAND OCCASIONS

The Concert Hall

Birgit Nilsson, the distinguished Swedish soprano, appeared in a Wagner programme and saluted the new Opera House with Elizabeth's Greeting from Tannhäuser, Dear Hall of Song.

Left. Tenor Robert Gard, described as 'a telling Anatol Kuragin' in Prokofiev's War and Peace.

This, "without question, must be the most innovative, the most daring, the most dramatic and in many ways the most beautiful home constructed for the lyric and related muses in modern times," wrote Martin Bernheimer of the Los Angeles Times after reviewing the premiere performances. Edward Greenfield of the London Guardian reported that the sails of the roofs "shine with a brilliance to make you blink. Catch them as I did for the first time against a glaring midday sun from the north across the harbour and the result is dazzling," he said. "Utzon's grand spinnaker structure, confronting the waterfront breeze, hits you like a monumental cluster of divine sailing boats," reported William Mann of The Times, London. "There were many who said that it would never work: some no doubt who will continue to say so even though it manifestly does," said Desmond Shawe-Taylor of the Sunday Times. "This is not, emphatically not, the white elephant the Jonahs have been predicting..." insisted the London Guardian's Edward Greenfield. He even chided those with lingering doubts. "I am tempted to say that Sydney does not deserve the Opera House at all, except that I suspect reactions will change..." Reactions did change — virtually overnight. The rapturous praise of visitors inspired everyone, especially artists and companies. They were determined the building would not steal all the thunder. Vast new audiences were attracted by reports of wonderful performances, as well as by reviews of a theatre complex of magical beauty.

On September 28, 1973 the premiere season began with a triumph — The Australian Opera's new production of Prokofiev's War and Peace. There was one empty seat in the Opera Theatre and on it a single rose. The seat had been paid for by a Chicago opera enthusiast. He was prevented from attending the premiere at the last moment and cabled instructions for the rose to be placed on his seat.

The next night the first Concert Hall performance was presented: a Wagner programme starring the Swedish soprano, Birgit Nilsson. She appeared with the Sydney Symphony Orchestra and a "homegrown guest hero", the visiting Australian conductor, Sir Charles Mackerras.

Sir Charles Mackerras conducted the first of the 1973 opening performances in the Concert Hall and has conducted regularly ever since. He was appointed chief conductor of the Sydney Symphony Orchestra in 1982 and is the first Australian to hold the post.

Above. The Australian baritone, Raymond Myers, as Napoleon in Prokofiev's War and Peace. The opera, premiered in the Opera Theatre by the Australian Opera on September 28, 1973, was enthusiastically received by Australian and visiting critics. Far left. Tenor Tom McDonnell sings as an impassioned Prince Andrei Bolkonsky. Left. The Australian soprano, Eilene Hannan, who appeared as Natasha 'stood out' wrote a critic, 'for a sweet candour of tone and bearing that was wholly and delectably right in the role.'

The concert began before a packed house, with the stirring overture to The Mastersingers, followed by the entrance of the beaming and imposing Miss Nilsson to begin her programme with Elisabeth's greeting from Tannhäuser: Dear Hall of Song.

Reviewing the performance, the Guardian's Edward Greenfield reported: "If any hall of song deserved to be greeted by the most triumphant Wagnerian soprano of our age it was surely the new Concert Hall of Sydney Opera House" — they were words that brought joy and relief to everyone associated with the Opera House.

But there was simply no time to dwell on the past. It was difficult enough keeping up with the arrival of the stars, the spectaculars that followed one after the other and the local and overseas reviews.

The bubbling, irreverent Nilsson, was everyone's darling. She was reminded during an interview that the conductor, Herbert von Karajan, with whom she had been feuding for years, had once accused her of "having a safe where her heart should be". "I am delighted that we have something in common," she retorted.

Administrators rushed to entertain her and the critics worshipped her. "That Birgit Nilsson can fill Valhalla with the might of her soprano voice we heard at first hand very recently," eulogised Fred Blanks of The Sydney Morning Herald. "That she can also convey tender and delicate songs with the adroitness of a Scandinavian troll became evident at her recital . . ." Incredible! Even the critics were proving poetic.

The second Concert Hall performance was given on Sunday afternoon, October 30, by the German Bach Soloists and a young Australian soprano, Marilyn Richardson. Later that day, the first of the Sunday Night at the Opera House variety shows was presented, with Rolf Harris topping the bill, and the next morning one of the world's most distinguished conductors, Lorin Maazel, and The Cleveland Orchestra moved in to rehearse for four Concert Hall performances. One of these featured Nilsson as soloist singing arias from Beethoven's Fidelio and Richard Strauss's Salome. Women staff members, enamoured of the handsome Maazel, found plenty of excuses to walk past the conductor's dressing room.

The Cleveland Orchestra's series was interspersed with an early evening concert for young people, presented entirely by Australians: the Sydney Symphony Orchestra, conducted by Patrick Thomas, with the enfant terrible Roger Woodward, the pianist as soloist. The programme included the Piano Concerto No 5 by Prokofiev.

During these initial performances entrepreneurs were dashing to the airport to welcome stars of England's D'Oyly Carte Opera Company and Petula Clark, who were among the artists who appeared in the Concert Hall during the second week of the season. The exhilarating pace of life at the Opera house had begun. Programmes were constantly

The Australian entertainer, Rolf Harris, was the first artist from the light entertainment world to appear at the Opera House. He was the star of Jack Neary's Sunday Night at the Opera House on September 30, 1973.

The Australian pianist, Roger Woodward, is a superb interpreter of many master works. He made his Opera House debut during the first season and has appeared repeatedly in the Concert Hall in subsequent triumphant seasons.

changing in all the halls: the Opera Theatre, the Drama Theatre, the Music Room and the Recording Hall. Exhibitions were being mounted, there were fashion parades in the foyers. Strollers thronged the promenade. There were queues at the box office and the guided tours desk; a continual round of late night receptions in the foyers and the boardroom. Couturiers and department store executives were blowing kisses in the direction of the Opera House. Women were buying as many as six dresses at a time for the premieres and parties. Fashion magazines were continually photographing mannequins and society leaders in their latest creations against the backdrop of the complex.

With the climax of the opening season imminent, the headlines ran "The Queen will be the star". The Queen's appearance in Sydney to open the Opera House was her first as "Queen of Australia". A few months earlier, on Good Friday, 1973, the then newly-elected Australian Labor Prime Minister, Gough Whitlam, was received by the Queen at Windsor Castle, where she consented to his government's request that she assume a new royal title when visiting Australia: "Elizabeth II, by the Grace of God, Queen of Australia and Her Other Realms and Territories, Head of the Commonwealth." The official opening ceremony took place outdoors in the Opera House forecourt on the afternoon of Saturday, October 20, 1973. Prayers were answered. The day was warm and sunny — but there were gale force winds. "The Queen's hemlines are weighted," confided her lady-in-waiting, Lady Susan Hussey, but the Queen was reported to have recalled that she had trouble keeping her hat on and her notes from flying away.

The ceremony was telecast direct around Australia and to the United Kingdom, Europe and New Zealand. Eight outside broadcast cameras were stationed around the Opera House and groups of photographers and journalists stood at vantage points. Even the republicans had to admit it: no one but the Queen would have attracted so much publicity or moved thousands of Sydney people to forego an afternoon at the beach or the races to line the streets and foreshores and engulf the Opera House.

After the Queen's speech, the royal party was taken on a tour of the complex. The Australian artist, John Coburn, stood waiting in the Opera Theatre, ready to explain the symbolism of his Curtain of the Sun, and in the foyer of the Concert Hall another artist, John Olsen, was waiting to answer royal questions about his mural, Salute to Slessor's Five Bells, inspired by the poet's elegy to his lost friend, Joe Lynch, and which has the waters of Sydney Harbour as its theme.

The Queen and the Duke of Edinburgh returned in the evening — as fireworks cascaded over the Opera House — for the "Royal Opening Concert". An American wrote offering any price demanded — he suggested $25,000 a seat — for ten tickets to the performance. He made

Left. After a pageant in the forecourt and the royal party's guided tour, the Opera House was launched like a ship on the official opening day. As the International Herald Tribune reported: 'Nylon streamers led from the highest peak of the roofs to four decorated tugs in the harbour. At a signal "Anchors away!", the tugs pulled the streamers apart. Simultaneously, hundreds of vessels in the harbour sounded whistles and horns and 60,000 balloons shot skywards.' Meanwhile, pigeons were released, F111 aircraft zoomed overhead and helicopters flew under the bridge. The celebrations were organized by the ebullient Sydney businessman, Sir Asher Joel. He was then a member of the New South Wales Government and the Sydney Opera House Trust.

Gough Whitlam, Australia's first Labor Prime Minister for 23 years, is a distinguished scholar as well as politician, and a regular patron of the arts.

The royal party on the promenade after the opening festivities. The Aboriginal actor, Ben Blakeney, stood stoically on the highest roof representing the 'spirit of Bennelong'; but Bennelong's speech was spoken by another actor, James Condon. Blakeney was feted by admirers after his performance but, as a critic said later, he was merely 'king for a day' and he has not been invited to appear at the Opera House since.

one proviso: his guests should join the Queen for supper afterwards. His offer was declined by the New South Wales Government. The tickets were priceless. Admission was by invitation only.

The concert began with Jubugalee — a musical flourish by the Australian composer, John Antill. The major work was Beethoven's Symphony No 9 in D minor, "The Choral". This great "symphonic sermon on the mount" was performed by the Sydney Symphony Orchestra, the Sydney Philharmonia Choir and the Sydney Philharmonia Motet Choir, conducted by the late Dutch maestro, Willem van Otterloo, who was then chief conductor of the Sydney Symphony Orchestra. The Australian soloists were the tenor, Ronald Dowd, the contralto, Lauris Elms, the soprano, Nance Grant, and the baritone, Raymond Myers.

During their three-day tour for the opening the Queen and the Duke of Edinburgh visited the complex several times and attended a performance of Mozart's The Magic Flute in the Opera Theatre on Monday, October 22, 1973. The previous Sunday they had walked down to the building through the Royal Botanic Gardens from the neighbouring Government House to see the exhibition, All The World's A Stage, watch a rehearsal of Berthold Brecht's The Three-penny Opera and tour backstage. Here they were escorted by the technical director, Willi Ulmer, a Bavarian who speaks excellent English but who explained the finer points of the stage machinery to the Duke in German, and became a devoted admirer of the Queen. A few months later, in February, 1974, when a protocol officer was questioning Ulmer's arrangements for a backstage tour by Princess Anne, the

Bruce Martin and Joan Sutherland in a 1982 Concert Hall performance of Donizetti's Lucrezia Borgia. The Australian Opera first presented this work at the Opera House in 1977, when it was produced in the Opera Theatre with Sutherland in the title role.

volatile German exploded. The Queen had been perfectly happy to take things as she found them. "If it was good enough for the mother, it will be good enough for the daughter," he declared.

Royal visits are one thing; great performances another. People are always asking who has given the most successful performance — but there have been so many great performances, so many capacity houses, so much wild acclaim. Who will ever forget Joan Sutherland being mobbed at the Opera House by fans and reporters in 1974, when she returned to Australia for the first time in nine years? Initially, she was to appear in the first performance in the house but she found she was already committed to overseas engagements by the time the date of the premiere season was certain.

Sutherland made her Opera House debut in recital in the Concert Hall on July 6, 1974. In a programme of songs by Rossini, Bellini, Donizetti, Massenet and other favourite composers, she was accompanied by her husband, Richard Bonynge at the piano. There had been such a scramble for tickets for that concert, the atmosphere was electric. The audience waited breathlessly for her first entrance. "Better than ever!" was the verdict of fans. "A professional!" they enthused backstage. "Always on time for rehearsals, always well prepared."

Sutherland's great achievements in the Concert Hall have included performances in Donizetti's Lucia di Lammermoor, Verdi's Otello and Donizetti's Lucrezia Borgia. "A national treasure! The finest jewel in our national crown," wrote enthralled critics — and no one will need reminding of her sensational recent concert with her frequent operatic partner, Luciano Pavarotti, which was televised direct internationally.

Above. Baritone, John Pringle, as Papageno, tenor, Anson Austin, as Tamino and Kathleen Moore, Rosemary Gunn and Etela Piha as the Queen of the Night's attendants in a 1980 performance of The Magic Flute in the Opera Theatre. Far left. The Australian soprano, Glenys Fowles, as Pamina in the same production. The opera was first presented in the Opera Theatre in 1973, when the Queen and the Duke of Edinburgh were in the audience and the soprano, Joan Carden appeared as Pamina. The Australian Opera has presented the opera several times since. Left. The Magic Flute with tenor, Anson Austin as Tamino and bass, Bruce Martin, as Sarastro.

They queued all night, camping on the Opera House concourse, for $5 standing room tickets for that January 23, 1983 performance. Seats, from $20 to $150, were over-subscribed immediately they were offered. Yet when Sutherland and Pavarotti first appeared together in Australia in 1965, in the national Sutherland-Williamson opera tour, Pavarotti was virtually unknown, and his performances without Sutherland were not well attended!

Right. Bonynge, Sutherland and Pavarotti acknowledge the plaudits after the 'Concert of the Century' on Sunday, January 23, 1983. Presented in the Concert Hall by the Australian Opera, it was broadcast direct internationally by the Australian Broadcasting Commission. The stars appeared with the Elizabethan Sydney Orchestra. Concertmaster, Ladislav Jasek, also appeared as a soloist.

Maria Prerauer, the arts editor of The Australian, the only national newspaper, is a perceptive and sometimes acerbic critic of the Australian Opera.

Stanislaw Skrowaczewski, the Polish conductor, electrified audiences with the Sydney Symphony Orchestra under his baton. The Opera House deeply moved the conductor who is also noted as a composer.

By contrast the "house full" signs were out for the two performances given by Leonard Bernstein and the New York Philharmonic Orchestra on August 22 and 23, 1974. On hearing that many people had been unable to obtain or afford tickets, Bernstein invited the public to the rehearsal on the morning of the second concert. The news was announced on radio at breakfast time. Within minutes the Concert Hall was inundated. With no advance warning of this open rehearsal, nor time to roster front-of-house staff, even the general manager deputized as an usher. At the end of the rehearsal, Bernstein invited the children present to come on stage to meet the orchestra which Maria Prerauer the Sydney Sunday Telegraph's arts editor has described as having "every member — a master musician".

The Sydney Symphony Orchestra has given many inspiring performances in the Concert Hall but none so fine, in the opinion of music critic, Professor Roger Covell, as those given in October and November, 1981 under the direction of the Polish composer and conductor, Stanislaw Skrowaczewski — renowned for his "scrupulous preparation". His programme included the monumental Symphony No 9 by Bruckner, the Symphony No 5 by Beethoven, The Magical Mandarin Suite by Bartok, and the Prelude and Liebestod from Wagner's Tristan and Isolde. "Listen to the silence," marvelled the maestro as he stood in the deserted, darkened Concert Hall after midnight, while touring the Opera House following his final concert.

Zubin Mehta also conducted the Israel Philharmonic Orchestra's three concerts at the Opera House in March, 1978. It was rumoured that every member of that orchestra carried a gun for protection. The management certainly feared terrorist attacks. Security precautions had not been so stringent since the official opening by the Queen. But concertgoers, who included many members of Sydney's Jewish community, were undaunted. They could not be persuaded to go home!

Ovation followed ovation after the last work in the series — the Symphony No 5 by Mahler. The conductor constantly returned to the platform but there was no fitting encore. It would have been superfluous — sacrilegious even — to attempt to embellish the lingering cry of anguish and regret that is the "Mahler five".

Maxim Shostakovich, son of the great Russian composer, was on tour in Australia when his father died. Conducting his father's symphony No. 10 after the event proved an experience deep with emotion.

Indian-born Zubin Mehta conducted the 110-strong Israel Philharmonic in three concerts in March 1978. Left, a section of the orchestra plays Mozart. The visit was supported by the Australian Broadcasting Commission and the Jewish community.

The Russian composer, Dimitri Shostakovich, died in August, 1975, while his son Maxim was fulfilling conducting engagements in Australia. The young conductor interrupted his tour to fly home for the funeral but he resumed a few days later with concerts at the Opera House with the Sydney Symphony Orchestra. His final programme in the Concert Hall ended with a reading of his father's Symphony No 10. It was an unbearably moving occasion. By the end of the performance music lovers felt in need of consolation themselves. Yet they rallied magnificently — standing to applaud as the grief-stricken conductor returned to the platform. He did not take a bow. He simply took the score from the rostrum, pressed it to his heart, and held it aloft in tribute to the dead composer.

Concertgoers around the world have often wondered if annotations in printed programmes are written to confound, rather than enlighten. "The second movement is a trio for nine tomtoms and pod rattle," runs a bewildering note about music for piano and percussion by

Right. The Sydney Philharmonia Society in rehearsal under its conductor, Peter Seymour, preparing for a performance of Bach's St. John Passion. The Society includes a smaller motet choir and in this work, was accompanied by the Sydney Philharmonia Orchestra.

Aaron Copland, the boy from Brooklyn, both composer and conductor, has shown that serious music can draw on sources as unexpected as jazz and cowboy songs.

The Italian maestro, Carlo Felice Cillario, who regularly conducts in both the Concert Hall and the Opera Theatre. Other conductors who have appeared at the Opera House include Franz-Paul Decker, Sir Charles Groves, John Hopkins, Hiroyuki Iwaki, Leif Segerstam, Jose Serebrier and Niklaus Wyss.

the contemporary American composer, John Cage. Yet the programme notes prepared by the Shanghai Philharmonic Society for its Concert Hall performances in November, 1975 were plain and brief. Summing up the song, No Difficulties Can Daunt a Communist, from the opera, The Red Lantern, which was presented by the impressive tenor, Hu Sung-hua, the programme explained: "This passage sung by railway worker and underground Party member in the opera, Li Yu-ho, expresses his loyalty to the Party and his readiness to sacrifice himself to the Party's cause." A song called "We Will Always Remember Chairman Mao's Kindness" was also presented, but the principal items on the programme were arias from a work composed collectively by members of the Shanghai Philharmonic Society: the "Revolutionary Symphony," Taking Tiger Mountain by Strategy. An instrumental item, "The Mobile State Shop Arrives in the Hill Village" featured a trumpet-like instrument, the suona. There was also fascinating music for the ancient Chinese wind instrument, the sheng; a bowed erhu, and for the plucked instruments — the pipa, the cheng, and the chin.

The Australian Opera's first production in the Concert Hall — Verdi's Aida — in January, 1975 proved that grand opera could be presented triumphantly in the hall — and that in conductor, Carlo Felice Cillario the season was under the direction of one of the great interpreters of Verdi. "Puccini makes you cry," he said. "Verdi breaks your heart."

Cillario has directed many of the most highly-acclaimed performances at the Opera House. "The Concert Hall seemed halfway lifted between heaven and earth," wrote critic, Hans Forst, after the November 19, 1981 performance of Verdi's Requiem presented by the Sydney Philharmonia Society, conducted by Cillario. The soloists were the soprano, Joan Carden, the contralto, Lauris Elms, the tenor, Anthony Benfell, and the bass, Noel Mangin.

Another great occasion was the concert version of Wagner's epic Parsifal presented in the Concert Hall on April 2, 1977. Cillario conducted forces drawn from the Sydney Symphony Orchestra, the Sydney Philharmonia Choir, boys of the Sydney Grammar School Choir, and stars of The Australian Opera, who were joined by the fine American bass, Reid Bunger in the role of Klingsor. This six and a half hour long performance began at 4 pm. At 6 pm, when the Opera House was still bathed in autumn sunshine, there was a 90-minute dinner interval. Patrons without restaurant reservations brought hampers instead, and had picnics out on the promenade. The hampers had been checked in at the cloakroom in their hundreds prior to the performance.

The presentation of all four operas which make up Wagner's monumental The Ring of the Nibelung was completed at the Opera House in 1983, when The Australian Opera presented a fully-staged production of The Valkyrie in the Opera Theatre with Cillario conducting and the English soprano, Rita Hunter, heading the cast. Presentation of the cycle began in 1979 with a fine concert version of The Rhinegold in the Concert Hall, conducted by the young Englishman, Mark Elder. In 1981 two concert performances of Twilight of the Gods, conducted by Sir Charles Mackerras, were presented in the hall. Rita Hunter appeared as Brunnhilde and the Australian tenor, Jon Weaving as Siegfried. Even more successful were the Concert Hall performances of Tristan and Isolde directed by Mackerras in 1982, with the English tenor, Alberto Remedios as Tristan and Hunter as Isolde.

Australian artists like Nellie Melba, Joan Sutherland and June Bronhill, once had to go overseas to find opportunities to work in opera. Now many opera stars come to Australia. Rita Hunter has even settled in Sydney. While everyone worries about her weight and her predilection for buns and soft drinks, she is one of the most beloved of all Opera House artists. Her good humour is legendary and she is given to practical jokes. During a performance of Verdi's Nabucco in the Concert Hall she replaced the phial of poison with a jar containing her gall stones, recently removed.

Impossible to imagine the regal American soprano, Jessye Norman, indulging in such practical jokes. She was not well-known in Australia when she made her first appearances in the Concert Hall with the Sydney Symphony Orchestra and in recital in 1976, but the ecstatic reception of her small audience and the critics ensured packed houses when she returned as "the Norman Conqueror" in 1981. "No one can reasonably expect finer singing this side of paradise," wrote Fred Blanks after her recital of songs by Haydn, Berg, and Richard Strauss, and encores which included Swing Low Sweet Chariot.

Music critic, Fred Blanks whose reviews appear in the Sydney Morning Herald.

The 'Norman Conqueror', Jessye Norman, who gave Concert Hall performances in 1976 and 1981 and took Sydney by storm.

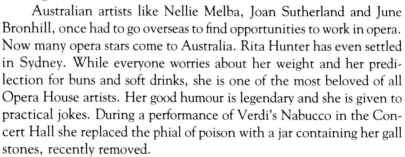

Right. A scene from Verdi's Aida, performed in the Concert Hall on January 30, 1975. The summer seasons of 1976 and 1977 saw its success repeated to full and enthusiastic houses. It was grand opera par excellence.

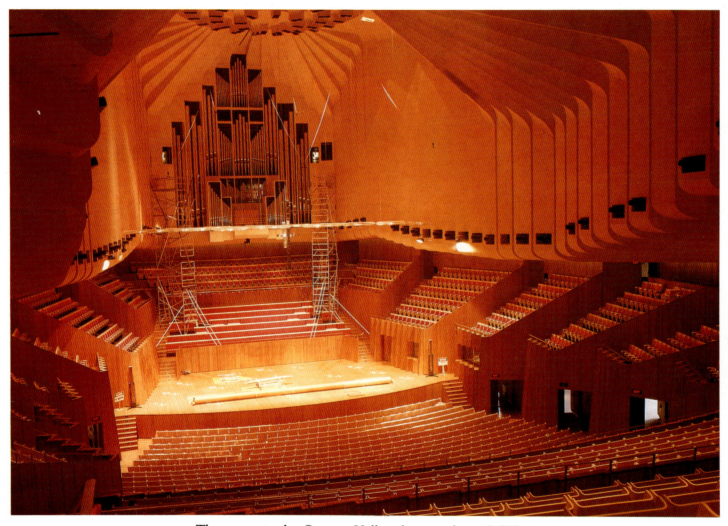

The organ in the Concert Hall with more than 10,000 pipes is another conquest. It is believed to be the largest mechanical-action organ in the world. The history of its construction, detailed in the Sydney Opera House Grand Organ booklet, was almost as controversial as that of the Opera House itself, but the premiere performance on the instrument on June 7, 1979 was a triumph for its self-taught designer and builder, the Australian Ronald Sharp. "Ronald Sharp had a dream of an organ for the Opera House that would sing with a thousand soft and stormy voices," began a leader in The Sydney Morning Herald on June 16, 1979. "After 10 years' work, he has realised that dream. The organ has played for the people of Sydney. Our music critic, Roger Covell, believes it has grace, power and clarity . . . Its soaring sound will fill the Concert Hall and live in the minds of those who hear it." They heard the organ in Europe as well as in Sydney in March, 1981 when, at

Until the completion of the Grand Organ in May 1979 the Concert Hall lacked its crowning feature. It was first given a public hearing on 7 June 1979.

the request of the European Broadcasting Union, a concert featuring the great organ symphony of Saint-Säens, the Symphony No 3, was broadcast direct. The Australian organist, Michael Dudman, was the soloist. He appeared with the Sydney Symphony Orchestra, conducted by the French maestro, Louis Fremaux. The world premiere of Symphony by the Australian composer, Nigel Butterley, was also on the programme.

The Concert Hall is also the scene of great choral works, as traditional as Handel's Messiah and Bach's Christmas Oratorio, or as avant-garde as Carmina Burana by Carl Orff.

The Sydney-born organ-builder, Ronald Sharp, designed and built the Grand Organ in the Concert Hall. He is pictured here tuning some of the instrument's 10,000 pipes. The organ has six departments and features a wide variety of electrical, recording and communication aids. During a performance, the organist keeps in touch with the conductor and orchestra through two closed-circuit television screens. Sharp is self-taught but has pioneered the design of the first hand-made Australian instruments.

The Sydney Philharmonia which performs such works dates back to 1920, when it was formed by a group of music lovers living in the Hurlstone Park district of the city. Known as the Hurlstone Park Choral Society until 1969, its members are amateur singers from all walks of life. The choir has a strength of one hundred and sixty, made up of sopranos, tenors, bass-baritones, mezzo sopranos and altos. A smaller group of 30 singers comprise the Sydney Philharmonia Motet Choir which was formed in 1972. This group presents music of much smaller compass such as madrigals, part-songs, chapel music and music from the 'baroque' repertoire of the 17th and early 18th centuries. On occasions both choirs sing together and they were both featured, with the Sydney Symphony Orchestra and soloists, in the performance of Beethoven's monumental Choral Symphony during the Royal Opening Concert.

The choirs and the Sydney Symphony Orchestra are frequently associated. Their joint annual performances at the Opera House always include three December performances of Handel's Messiah to full houses and the third performance has audience participation. The choirs are administered by the Sydney Philharmonia Society, which has a staff of two, and which presents an annual subscription season at centres around Sydney. The Australian conductor, Peter Seymour, has been music director of both choirs since 1969. He is also The Australian Opera's chorus master and regularly conducts performances for that company as well.

Less serious programmes brought well-known names. "I love Opera House audiences," said Bob Hope on his appearance. "They start laughing when they buy the tickets." During an interview in Sydney the beloved star, Bette Davis, said she had been investigated by the FBI during the McCarthy era. "I understand that their report said I was a hyperthyroid with a heart of gold," she said. "I am not hyperthyroid and I do not have a heart of gold. What a dump," she snapped when she walked out on stage in the Concert Hall. There was a roar of welcome. Many in the capacity house would have paid good money just to see her legendary walk — and most of the audience of Davis fanatics knew her opening line was a quotation from one of her films — Beyond the Forest.

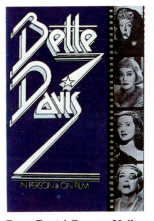

Bette Davis' Concert Hall appearances in March, 1975 were presented by Edgley and Dawe Attractions. Bob Hope, Don McLean and Roy Orbison were other stars who appeared during the 1975 season. Parry Como and Ronnie Corbett were headliners in 1976.

Above. The final curtain call at the Royal Charity Concert on May 27, 1980 when the Concert Hall at the Opera House was filled to capacity. Left. Peter Allen, Australian expatriate and versatile entertainer, performing at the Royal Charity Concert in 1980. Far left. Olivia Newton-John, popular singer whose residence is now in the United States but who enthusiastically returns to Australia.

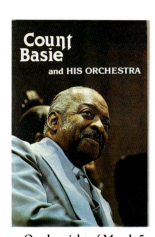

On the night of March 5, 1979 Count Basie And His Orchestra gave two Concert Hall performances — presented by the Australian Elizabethan Theatre Trust.

Sammy Davis Jnr. first appeared at the Opera House in 1977 for the Paradine Paterson organisation. He returned for a second season of full houses in 1979.

There was also exultation when it was announced that Ella Fitzgerald would give Concert Hall performances in November, 1978. During an interview in her dressing room she said "I love songs that have meaning. I like to sing lyrics that remind me of something in life." Asked if she had any unfulfilled ambitions, she said she would "like to make a beautiful album for children — seven to nine year-olds — lullabys and songs they love. Children are like flowers," she said. "They bud with love and attention." Count Basie — "a nobleman off stage and on" — gave Concert Hall performances with his orchestra on the night of March 5, 1979. Three days later, Peggy Lee was on stage singing You Give Me Fever and many of her other smash hits. Sammy Davis Jnr sang Mr. Bojangles during his show in the same year. Backstage he was always like a sultan surrounded by his retinue of aides.

The most widely celebrated variety show to date, however, was the Royal Charity Concert, presented in the Concert Hall on May 27, 1980 by an all-Australian cast in the presence of the Queen and the Duke of Edinburgh. The headliners were Julie Anthony, Peter Allen, Olivia Newton-John and Helen Reddy and the concert in aid of disabled people was televised direct around Australia. Tickets, from $10.50 to $50.50, sold out immediately, and all the artists gave their services free. The cast included the pop star, Johnny Farnham, the pianist, Roger Woodward, the ventriloquist, Chris Kirby, the comedians Bert Newton and Paul Hogan, members of The Australian Ballet and the Sydney Dance Company, the Australian International Orchestra and a massed choir, conducted by Tommy Tycho.

It was during rehearsals for this concert that room-service operated for the first time. Catering staff, as anxious as everyone else to meet the stars in person, were delighted to serve meals in the dressing rooms. Even so, it was remembered that Dame Joan and other divas always line up like everyone else at the Green Room canteen.

On other occasions, too, artists readily came forward to donate their services and in the Concert for Darwin, presented to aid victims of the devastating 1974 cyclone, the Australian soprano, June Bronhill, and Australia's favourite tenor, Donald Smith, were among the stars from all fields of the entertainment world. Full houses have been frequent in the Concert Hall and a record audience was attracted by the great Russian-born pianist, Vladimir Ashkenazy who gave a Chopin recital on December 7, 1982. With even standing room only sold out, Ashkenazy agreed to an extra 150 chairs being placed on stage. Proceeds from the concert went to aid micro-research, and Ashkenazy, who performed without fee, dedicated the recital to the notable Australian micro-surgeons who had successfully operated on his son and enabled him to resume a normal life. His leg had been almost severed during a holiday in Greece and there were fears it would have to be amputated.

'Ella never goes out of style' they say. Her Concert Hall performances in November, 1978 were presented by the Australian Elizabethan Theatre Trust.

The pianist, Vladimir Ashkenazy has toured Australia repeatedly for the Australian Broadcasting Commission, first appearing in 1969.

Other great pianists have also appeared in the Concert Hall, among them Claudio Arrau, Alfred Brendel, Jorge Bolet, Michele Campanella, Joerg Demus, John Ogden, Michael Ponti, Rudolf Serkin, Fou Ts'ong and Mark Zeltser. There have been many magnificent violinists too, Kyung-Wha Chung, Erich Gruenberg, Ida Haendel, Yehudi Menuhin, Henryk Szeryng, Wanda Wilkomirska and cellists have included the "god-like" Andre Navarra, Janos Starker and Paul Tortellier. James Galway, who played Irish airs on a tin whistle enchanted his audience with Mozart on a flute made of gold; and the classical guitar has filled the great hall with sound in the hands of such masters as Julian Bream, Alexandra Lagoya, John Williams and Narciso Yepes. "We had to play well, the acoustics are so good," said Arnaldo Apostoli of I Musici after the ensemble's Concert hall debut in July, 1976.

Those acoustics were further tested by the Quartetto Beethoven di Roma, the Amadeus Quartet, the Australian Chamber Orchestra, the Academy of St Martin-in-the-Fields, the Choir of King's College Cambridge and the Sydney String Quartet which the promoter, Musica Viva Australia, presented to enthusiastic music-lovers. But not only music has flooded the Concert Hall: great meetings have enlivened it, not least a lunch-time rally organized by the Australian Labor Party in 1974, shortly before the May 18 general election at which the party's mandate to govern was renewed. The line-up of 20 distinguished speakers on stage included the then Prime Minister, Gough Whitlam, the historian, Professor Manning Clark, the Aboriginal leader, Shirley Smith, playwright, David Williamson, actress, Kate Fitzpatrick and the Australian Nobel laureate, Patrick White, who described Gough Whitlam as "a man of vision", like the architect of the Opera House. The Prime Minister must not be allowed to be "sacrificed" as Utzon was, said White. There were, however, complaints that some of the speeches were too long. People had to get back to work. Someone in the foyer, disappointed that he had to leave before hearing a favourite speaker, cupped his hands to his mouth and called out "You couldn't run a barbecue".

The Australian guitarist, John Williams, regularly tours Australia as a celebrity artist. He made his Opera House debut in 1974 and has given several Concert Hall performances since.
Left. A Saturday afternoon matinee audience enjoying refreshments in the Opera Theatre foyer.

Yehudi Menuhin, the virtuoso violinist has visited Australia on a number of occasions throughout his life, most recently in the role of conductor.

ENTER PRIMA DONNAS
The Opera Theatre

The music of Richard Wagner has been performed since the 1973 opening season. Performance of all four operas in the composer's Ring of the Nibelung cycle was completed in 1983.

Left. Joan Sutherland as Violetta in John Copley's production of Verdi's La Traviata — 1981.

Richard Wagner's merciless exploitation of his most fervent and generous patron, Ludwig of Bavaria, led to the emotional and political destruction of the young king, and his financial ruin. Yet if Ludwig had not subsidized the composer, he may have been too distracted by financial worries to complete The Ring, or Parsifal, or build his famous Festspielhaus in Bayreuth.

No British sovereign has gone bankrupt because of a passion for opera. In fact, British royalty have tended to leave the business of commissioning items to enrich the musical repertoire to their counterparts across the Channel. Yet despite British royalty's comparatively poor record of patronage of the performing arts, veneration for British monarchs, especially in the present century, has inspired the establishment and led to the subsidization by the taxpayer of many great orchestras and companies: the Royal Philharmonic Orchestra and the Royal Opera to name just two. Similarly, the formation of several of Australia's national and state companies and orchestras was inspired by the Royal Tour of 1954. In the euphoria that followed, many ideas were put forward to commemorate the young Queen Elizabeth's visit, among them a suggestion that a government-funded organization should be established to promote opera, ballet and drama. As a result the Australian Elizabethan Theatre Trust was formed in 1956.

The national opera company, The Australian Opera, which now performs at the Opera House for seven months of the year, was one of the first companies established by the trust. Formed in 1956, it was known as the Elizabethan Trust Opera Company until 1970, when it became self-governing. Some of the foundation members of the company had previously appeared with the New South Wales National Opera Company, but this ensemble was a national company in name only. Formed in 1951 as the special project of the music patron and society hostess, Clarice Lorenz, it presented occasional seasons until the establishment of the government-funded national company.

Performances by both Clarice Lorenz's ensemble and the young Australian Opera are remembered with nostalgia. There were old

Ludwig II, King of Bavaria, not only beggared his country's treasury on fantastic castles and palaces, but also encouraged the musical aspirations of Richard Wagner.

shacks of theatres and cramped, tawdry dressing rooms to be endured and seasons rarely extended beyond a few weeks. Yet there was great camaraderie backstage and the promise of bigger and better things to come. There was talk of a Sydney Opera House — but only talk — artists had time to establish a repertoire and gain confidence before being subjected to the scrutiny of international critics and audiences.

The life of the young company was made even more interesting by the visits of internationally famous expatriate and foreign guest artists, among them the conductor, Karl Rankl, the sopranos Marie Collier and Elsie Morrison, the tenors Franco Brozessi, Kenneth Neate, Umberto Borso and Tito Gobbi, and the mezzo-soprano, Yvonne Minton. Not all the visitors lasted a season. An eminent conductor arrived — only to leave in great haste when he suddenly received an offer to appear with a famous diva in a grand house overseas. Yet the greatest divas appeared with The Australian Opera even in its infancy. The internationally beloved Australian soprano, Dame Joan Hammond, returned from overseas to appear with the company in 1957 in the role of Desdemona in Verdi's Otello and in the title role in Puccini's Tosca. She returned in 1961 as Salome in Richard Strauss's opera of that name and as Puccini's Madam Butterfly. Those performances are remembered as among the finest in the company's history.

The Opera Theatre which has 1,547 stalls, circle and box seats and sometimes displays the tapestry 'Curtain of the Sun' by the Australian artist, John Coburn, woven in Felletin, near Aubusson, France from Australian wool.

Above. Garth Welch and Kathleen Gorham in The Display. Robert Helpmann was commissioned to create the work for The Australian composer, Malcolm Williamson and is one of the most successful ballets in the company's repertoire. Above right. Peggy Sager as The Spirit of the Lost Umbrella and Helene Kirsova as Little Anna in a ballet by Kirsova, The Revolution of the Umbrellas, presented in 1943.

In 1956 television was introduced in Australia. It became a national pastime but there were nonetheless audiences for opera. Despite claims to the contrary, there has always been a following for opera in Australia. Even so, artists and administrators remember the audiences of the 1950's and 1960's with special affection. The theatres of the day were old and often shabby, yet opera lovers came in all weathers to encourage the young touring company. And what a trek it was for Sydney audiences! Until the opening of the Opera House, Sydney seasons were at the Elizabethan Theatre in a back street of Newtown. Those who set out on a rainy winter's evening to travel across town by train to the threadbare old theatre were opera-lovers indeed.

Although there has always been a following for opera in Australia, the popularity of the Opera House has helped to attract vast new audiences of Sydney people — and visitors from around the world. Before the building opened The Australian Opera presented an annual six-week Sydney season. It now presents an annual Opera House summer season in January and February and a winter season in the house extending from June to October. Performances are generally sold out from the stalls to standing room. The company's interstate and country touring commitments and the heavy demand for the Opera House theatres by other companies and orchestras prevent extensions of the opera seasons.

The Australian Opera performs at the Opera House with the Elizabethan Sydney Orchestra, which was formed like the company in 1956 by the Australian Elizabethan Theatre Trust, or the Australian Chamber Orchestra, which was formed in 1975 by the Australian conductor and cellist, John Painter. The company's vast repertoire includes three specially commissioned Australian operas, as well as works from the 18th, 19th and 20th centuries.

Above. Helene Kirsova as Columbine in Le Carnaval, a ballet presented in Australia by the touring Ballet Russe de Monte Carlo in 1936. Kirsova later returned to form her own ballet company. Based in Sydney, it included many European dancers stranded in Australia by the outbreak of World War II and was the first professional ensemble to be formed in Australia.

As Rites of Passage by the Australian composer, Peter Sculthorpe, could not be completed in time to be presented as The Australian Opera's first production at the Opera House, Prokofiev's War and Peace was chosen to replace it. The choice of a comparatively little-known Russian opera to open Australia's new Opera House startled many people. The music critic, Nadine Amadio, although approving the choice in an article in the Australian Financial Review, said she thought the man in the steet would have preferred a more popular opera, such as Verdi's Aida. War and Peace was selected because the opera's music director, Edward Downes, wanted to present a significant 20th century opera. Based on Tolstoy's novel about the futility of war, the opera has a cogent plot as well as an adventurous score. This epic work calls for a large cast, another factor in its selection. Every member of the company, with one exception, had a role in the historic premiere. Production and backstage harmony was assured. The only principal who did not appear was the tenor, Donald Smith, who was being held in reserve as the star of another production, Puccini's Il Trittico.

Author and music reviewer, Nadine Amadio.

Prior to the premiere of War and Peace a dress rehearsal was televised for overseas presentation by the British Broadcasting Corporation. Filming was held up briefly when two possums made an impromptu appearance on stage. Despite the ovation that greeted their debut, they fled. Before performances became regular events, possums from the Botanic Gardens often made nocturnal visits to the Opera House.

Reviewing the premiere itself, The Sydney Morning Herald's critic, Professor Roger Covell, wrote: 'With last night's opening performance of War and Peace in the Opera Theatre, the Australian Opera succeeded in demonstrating that Prokofiev's operatic selection from Tolstoy was an excellent choice for showing off both the ensemble abilities of the company and the capacity of the theatre to contain an ingeniously-produced work of spectacular dimensions...'

An opening season performance of Mozart's The Magic Flute took place in the presence of the Queen and the Duke of Edinburgh on October 22, 1973. It was a rare occasion. Two sovereigns appeared that night — Queen Elizabeth and Mozart's Queen of the Night — a role sung with understandable evidence of a 'fluttering vibrato' by the soprano, Chesne Ryman. What agonies of stage fright she must have suffered as she stood waiting to deliver her famous aria, acknowledged as one of the most demanding in the repertoire. Yet it was a 'Magic Flute with fun and style,' a 'dainty dish to set before the Queen of Australia'. To amuse her the producer, John Copley, took liberties with act one. The tenor, Anson Austin, as Tamino, was offered Australian delicacies — passionfruit and lamingtons — instead of the European sugar bread and figs specified in the libretto, and the wild African animals that Tamino usually enchants with his air on the flute were replaced by

David Ahern, the young music critic of the Sydney Daily Telegraph was a lone voice in praising Felix Werder's The Affair.

Above. Scene from Peter Sculthorpe's Rites of Passage performed in the Opera Theatre in 1974. Right. Scene from Felix Werder's one-act opera, The Affair, which has a libretto by the Melbourne writer, Leonard Radic. Werder was born in Berlin in 1922 and came to Australia in 1940. The Affair was commissioned by The Australian Opera in 1969 and was premiered in the Opera Theatre on March 14, 1974. Far right. Jacqueline Kensett-Smith and Robert Gard in The Affair, an opera which has not been repeated.

Above. Mikhail Barishnikov was brought to Australia by Michael Edgley, the entrepreneur. Above centre. Marcia Haydée and Richard Cragun in The Stuttgart Ballet's production of The Taming of the Shrew by John Cranko in October, 1974. Above left. Natalia Makarova who appeared with Ballet Victoria in the Opera Theatre in 1975. Left. Ron Stevens as Jakob Lenz and Grant Dickson as Pastor Oberlin in Larry Sitsky's one act-opera, Lenz. The libretto is by Gwen Harwood. The composer was born in China of Russian parents in 1934, and has lived in Australia since he was 17.

Australian children who came frisking and capering on stage, one dressed as a koala bear, another as a kangaroo, a third as a platypus and there was 'a spiny ant-eater' and 'a monkey'. This happy little menagerie was introduced to the Queen and the Duke backstage at interval. Charles Mackerras conducted the performance and the distinguished cast included the Australian soprano, Joan Carden — 'her Pamina must rank as one of her finest performances' — and the Australian bass, Donald Shanks — 'one of the most impressive-looking Sarastros ever to walk the stage.'

Another opening season production was Opera Through The Time Machine, designed to introduce children to opera. During the hour-long show, Robert Gard, as the Wizard of Op, became the first tenor in operatic history to make an entrance on roller skates. Initially, only one performance of Opera Through The Time Machine was scheduled, but the show became so popular it was presented again

There were failures, however, as well as successes during the opening season. In spite of the 'passionately sensual singing' of soprano, Elizabeth Connell, in Wagner's Tannhäuser, the production was condemned in a headline which read 'Sex show that fell flat', and as 'the last Tannhäuser in Paris' by conductor, Charles Mackerras, who was in the first night audience. The curtain rose to reveal a backdrop on which slides of 'swollen breasts, bottoms and female genitalia' were projected. 'Cold, clinical and a yawning bore,' commented music critic, Maria Prerauer. 'It was the sort of thing a slaughter of surgeons might show each other after dinner.' Another reviewer wrote: 'The projections intended by the producer, Bernd Benthaak, and the designer, Ralph Koltai, to depict an erotic inferno were likely to excite only the most avid subscriber to Penthouse. Gigantic colour reproductions of the female breast have an unfortunate tendency to resemble a dessert of cold blancmange topped with crystallised fruit.'

Some members of the audience walked out of the disappointing and 'long, long, long' production of Tannhäuser. Australian operagoers tend to signify their disappointment in that way. Yet when they do walk out of theatres, they generally do so quietly, almost regretfully. The same operagoers, unlike their counterparts in Europe and the United States, are rarely carried away to the point of giving twenty or thirty-minute ovations. But neither are they in the habit of booing or showing disapproval by more volatile means.

Complaints about Opera House seats are always more numerous after disappointing performances. Opinion about the comfort of the seats varies. The music critic, Fred Blanks, who by the beginning of 1983 had attended nine hundred and twenty performances in the complex, claims the seats are comfortable. Another critic, John Cargher, disagrees.

Music writer and broadcaster, John Cargher outside the Adelaide Festival Centre.

Elizabeth Connell, the distinguished soprano, has sung a number of leading roles with the Australian Opera, but none more memorable than in Jenufa.

101

Left. The American bass baritone, James Morris, left, appeared in the title role in The Australian Opera's 1978 performances of Mozart's Don Giovanni. He is seen here with Joan Carden as Donna Anna and Henri Wilden as Don Ottavio. Above. Scene from the Scottish Opera's production of Wagner's The Master-singers of Nuremberg, which was presented in the Opera Theatre in 1978 by The Australian Opera. Right. Robert Gard and Ronald Maconaghie, centre stage, as the brothers Palmieri in the 1977 production of Gilbert and Sullivan's The Gondoliers.

The Northern Foyer of the Opera Theatre offers 'magical' views of Sydney Harbour.

Australian critics and composers regularly complain that comparatively little new music is presented at the Opera House. They say that the building is a masterpiece of 20th century architecture, yet its music theatres are used primarily for the presentation of masterworks from the 18th and 19th century repertoires. Arts administrators who are attacked for their disinclination to experiment, point to the worldwide reluctance by audiences, sponsors — and many artists — to embrace contemporary music and claim that their companies would face bankruptcy if they continually programmed new works by unknown names.

Opera, in particular, is notoriously expensive to mount. All productions call for weeks of rehearsal and most require a large orchestra, a large cast and several changes of lavish costumes and sets. Even though the great standard works invariably attract capacity houses, box office receipts, despite high ticket prices, never cover production costs. To balance their books, companies around the world depend on large

Right. Henry Wilden as Hoffmann and Gordon Wilcock as the inventor, Spalunzani, in The Tales of Hoffmann by Offenbach. Joan Carden appeared in all four soprano roles during the 1980 season.

Edward Downes, musical director of The Australian Opera at the opening of the Sydney Opera House. He chose Prokofiev's War and Peace as the inaugural work.

The Australian Opera includes works by the late Benjamin Britten in its repertoire, the most successful, a presentation of A Midsummer Night's Dream.

government subsidies or the support of big business. The Australian Opera, like most of the companies which perform at the Opera House, receives financial assistance from both government sources and the private sector but as private sponsors can claim a tax rebate of forty-seven percent of their donations, the taxpaying community is primarily responsible for subsidizing the companies' performances.

The Australian Opera has presented and re-presented several operas by the 20th century composers Benjamin Britten and Leos Janácek with great success, but has produced no Australian opera since 1974. In that year, in addition to Sculthorpe's Rites of Passage, two one-act operas composed in Australia were given their world premieres: Larry Sitsky's Lenz and Felix Werder's The Affair.

Many critics were deeply impressed by Rites of Passage, but the general view was that it was providential that the work was not finished in time for presentation as the first Opera House attraction. The opera, also described as 'music theatre', 'music drama' and 'a dreadful dirge', is based on ancient Aboriginal rituals. Through music, dance and chants it depicts man's journey from birth through initiation, marriage and death to re-birth.

Sitsky's Lenz, based on the tragic life of the 19th century German poet, Jakob Lenz, was described by reviewers as 'an unmistakable masterwork', 'powerful and compelling' and as 'the best opera ever produced in Australia', but again the response of audiences was tepid. Alas! Werder's comedy, The Affair, set in an Australian Embassy in Europe, was extravagantly praised by no one except the Sydney Daily Telegraph's young critic, David Ahern.

The great successes of the 1974 season were The Tales of Hoffmann, by Offenbach, and Jenufa by Leos Janácek. Joan Sutherland made her first appearance with The Australian Opera on July 13, 1974 when she sang all four soprano roles in The Tales of Hoffmann. She did not disappoint, but 'brought the audience to the highest pitch of excitement', as she appeared by turns as Olympia the mechanical doll, Giulietta the Venetian courtesan, Antonia the ailing young singer, and Stella the prima donna. After the rapturous first-night curtain calls, the opera's general manager, John Winther, came on stage to announce that Joan Sutherland and her husband, Richard Bonynge, who had conducted 'Hoffmann' had agreed to become honorary members of the company. They returned to work with The Australian Opera in 1976, when Richard Bonynge replaced Edward Downes as musical director. Since then they have spent six months each year with the company.

The English producer, John Copley, who regularly works with The Australian Opera.

The surprise of the 1974 season was the warmth of the reception given to a Czechoslovakian opera new to Australia — Jenufa — a stark, melancholy work, composed by Janácek in 1904. It was premiered a few days after the opulent production of The Tales of Hoffmann. The performances of a young company member, the soprano, Elizabeth Connell, in the role of the stepmother, Kostelnicka, were judged by Roger Covell to have 'decisively surpassed' those of her counterpart, 'the illustrious Kerstin Meyer' in a production of Jenufa in Stockholm the same year. But critics were so overwhelmed by the successive Opera House triumphs they hardly seemed to know whom to praise most. Writing in The National Times, Kevon Kemp said: 'While everyone was looking to the current Joan Sutherland season of Tales of Hoffmann to put a shine on the next two or three years of opera-going, the ranging talents of conductor, Edward Downes, producer John Copley and the Australian Opera itself were preparing a shock event — the Janácek opera, Jenufa. With a little perspective on it now, after a week's run of time, it seems to me that Jenufa is not only the triumph of this present Australian Opera season but the most arching achievement of all the company's seasons so far.'

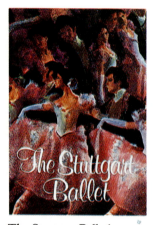

The Stuttgart Ballet's 1974 Australian tour was arranged by Edgley and Dawe Attractions, J.C. Williamson Theatres and the Australian Elizabethan Theatre Trust.

Other press clippings reveal that the company began its 1975 season with the Sydney premiere of Kurt Weill's The Rise And Fall Of The City Of Mahagonny. A cabaret opera set in 1929, it has a harsh, provocative libretto by Bertolt Brecht, and sets out to prove that despite the posturing and protestations of society, poverty is considered the greatest crime. A young set designer from The Australian Opera, Vicki Feitscher, bought costumes for the cast of pimps, prostitutes, gangsters and gamblers from a selection of vintage suits, hats and dresses in a suburban St Vincent de Paul Society charity shop. Meanwhile, other members of the opera's wardrobe department were busy completing the sumptuous costumes for Verdi's Aida. 'Mahagonny' was

Above. Scene from The Australian Ballet's 1978 production of Spartacus with Kelvin Coe, left, as the Roman commander, Crassus.

Right. Gary Norman in the title role of Spartacus and Marilyn Rowe Maver as his wife, Flavia, in The Australian Ballet's 1978 production of the work, created by the Hungarian, László Seregi, with music by Aram Khachaturian.

Soprano, Joan Carden, as the consumptive courtesan, Violetta, in Verdi's La Traviata — The Fallen Woman — Opera Theatre, 1979. Kiri Te Kanawa and Joan Sutherland have also appeared in this role with The Australian Opera.

generally well received. 'Lone Koppel Winther turned in her best performance yet as the tarty but occasionally loving Jenny,' wrote critic, Frank Harris. 'Her Alabamah Song, the most famous in the opera, was beautifully expressive, sad and moving in its mood of longing.' Georg Tintner conducted the opera. During the 1975 season he also conducted Beethoven's Fidelio. 'The conductor's saintly white mop of hair tossed like a dandelion puffball in the powerful breeze of his extraordinarily energetic movements in the pit,' wrote Roger Covell. 'Vocally,' he said, 'the performance was one of the most rewarding evenings the Australian Opera has provided this season. Ronald Dowd sounded in clearer, firmer, more heroically anguished voice than ever; Raymond Myers was a brilliantly resounding Pizarro and was all the more credible a villain for having the brisk manner of a busy bureaucrat; Robert Allman made a much more vocally imposing figure out of the Minister of State than happens in many a performance of this opera . . .'

1976 was the year the New Zealand-born soprano, Kiri Te Kanawa, 'always a handsome presence on stage,' made her Australian Opera debut 'in luminous voice' as Amelia in Verdi's Simone Bocca-

Cynthia Johnston as Barena, Lone Koppel Winther as Jenufa and Rosina Raisbeck as Grandmother Buryia in Janacek's Jenufa — Opera Theatre, 1980. The work was first presented by The Australian Opera, with Elizabeth Connell in the title role, in 1974.

negra. During the season she also appeared as a guest artist in the role of Mimi in Puccini's La Bohême, although a resident principal, Etela Piha, as Musetta, almost outshone her. Piha 'was all minx', said a critic. 'She brought the audience to the point of cheering.' The 1976 season closed with sparkling performances by 'two great Australian troupers,' June Bronhill and Dennis Olsen, in Gilbert and Sullivan's comic operas HMS Pinafore and Iolanthe.

In 1977 the young American soprano, Leona Mitchell reduced audiences to tears when she made her debut with The Australian Opera as Madam Butterfly. 'How could Pinkerton ever bring himself to leave her?' wondered the Bulletin's Brian Hoad. During 1976 Sutherland appeared in the oriental extravaganza, Lakmé, by Delibes, and a young Scottish soprano, Isobel Buchanan, then only twenty-one, was engaged as a member of the company. She made her debut as Pamina in The Magic Flute. Later in 1976 she eclipsed a visiting star when she sang the supporting role of Micaela in Bizet's Carmen. As predicted, Isobel Buchanan is now in great demand internationally. She is married to the Australian actor, Jonathan Hyde. They met in 1978 when they appeared together in The Australian Opera's first and immensely successful production of Benjamin Britten's A Midsummer Night's Dream.

Bellini's Norma, with Sutherland in the title role, was also presented during the 1978 season. The Australian mezzo-soprano, Margreta Elkins, appeared as the priestess, Adalgsia. Although Elkins is widely regarded as one of the world's best singers, she rarely appears in a leading role. Very few leading roles have been written for a mezzo-soprano. Bizet's Carmen and Saint-Saëns's Delilah are notable exceptions. The poor mezzo is nearly always the bridesmaid, if not the groom. With the demise of the castrati, mezzo-sopranos are now allotted the numerous 'trouser roles', such as the young warrior lover, Idamante in Mozart's Idomeneo.

Wagner's comedy, The Mastersingers of Nuremberg, was also on the 1978 programme. Costumes and sets for the production, the first of the opera to be seen in Australia for 'more than two generations,' were lent by the Scottish Opera, because the Australian company's then general manager, Peter Hemmings, formerly the head of the Scottish company, believed that sharing productions could reduce the cost of opera internationally. The cast and the production team included artists from both the Australian and Scottish companies. A young Englishman, Mark Elder, conducted. The visiting bass, Norman Bailey, in the leading role of Hans Sachs, was well received, but not so highly praised as the Australian soprano, Marilyn Richardson, as Eva. A 'crisply blanched and braided German maiden,' she sang with 'great strength and beauty'. She was 'outstanding' said John Carmody of The National Times. 'As always, she acted with riveting conviction.'

Left. The Australian Ballet performed the tragic tale of Anna Karenina in 1979, to music by Tchaikovsky. Above. Marilyn Rowe Maver dances as Anna, and Gary Norman as Vronsky. Above right. A moment of tension in the 1978 Australian Opera production of A Midsummer Night's Dream, composed by Benjamin Britten. Right. Mark Brinkley and Christine Walsh in Peggy van Praagh's production of Coppélia by the Australian Ballet in 1979.

Above. Scene from The Australian Opera's 1980 production of Verdi's Nabucco. The company first presented the work in the Opera Theatre during the 1973 opening season and in 1978 it was presented in the Concert Hall. Far left. Elizabeth Fretwell, Alan Light and Donald Solomon in Rossini's The Barber of Seville. Left. Glenys Fowles and John Pringle in John Cox's production of Rossini's The Barber of Seville. Right. David Burch and Janne Blanch of The Australian Ballet in Rudolf Nureyev's production of Don Quixote — Opera Theatre, 1979.

But perhaps the most significant event of 1978 was the enlargement, early in the year, of the Opera Theatre's orchestral pit. From the time of the opening season it was obvious that 'grand opera' could be successfully presented in the theatre. Even so, conductors, critics and administrators were convinced that the enlargement of the pit would enable grand opera to be presented there even more successfully. Originally, the pit accommodated a maximum of sixty musicians. With its enlargement under the stage, space was made for another twenty players. The pit could not be extended into the area of the stalls without jeopardizing the cables, which lie below the first row of seats, and which help to anchor the building's sail roofs. The extension work was carried out under the supervision of Willi Ulmer, who was then the Opera House's technical director. The project, years in the planning, took only three months to execute. The renovations did not make the pit ideal, of course. Some operas and ballets demand an orchestra of one hundred and twenty, but most works can be adequately presented with a musical force of eighty. In fact, many operas call for a smaller ensemble. Operas and ballets which do require a very large orchestra are presented in the Concert Hall.

The 'first of the spaghetti westerns', Puccini's The Girl of the Golden West, was a highlight of the 1979 season. The American soprano, Marilyn Zschau, standing in at the last minute for her ailing compatriot, Carol Neblett, made an impressive Australian Opera debut as Minnie in this production, and the Australian tenor, Donald Smith, as Dick Johnson, alias the bandit Ramerrez, 'established himself with ringing authenticity as a Puccinian tenor hero from his first entrance.'

Performances of an early Verdi opera, I Masnadieri — The Robbers — starring Joan Sutherland and Donald Smith were scheduled for the winter of 1980. Opera-goers were looking forward to seeing Australia's most famous soprano and its best-loved tenor together for the first time. Alas! Despite Smith's 'robust' singing during the first night gala premiere, it was announced next day that the tenor, battling ill-health for some time, would retire immediately from the operatic stage.

The consensus was that the 'towering achievements' of the 1980 season were the productions of Janáček's Katya Kabanova and Mussorgsky's masterpiece, Boris Godunov. 'It's not just Godunov — it's superb!' ran the headline over Maria Prerauer's review. 'Katya' was conducted by Mark Elder, produced by David Poutney and starred Marilyn Richardson in the title role. 'Boris' was conducted by Elgar Howarth, staged by Elijah Moshinsky and starred Donald Shanks.

Verdi's Macbeth, conducted by Mackerras, with Robert Allman in the title role and Rita Hunter as his lady was one of the successes of the 1981 season. Meyerbeer's Les Huguenots was also presented that year. In spite of the sumptuous costumes and sets and Joan Sutherland's

Programme designed by David Colville and Beryl Green for Mussorgsky's Boris Godunov presented in both 1980 and 1982.

Leos Janacek, the Czech composer, only achieved recognition as an opera composer in the 1960's. His work, Jenufa, took Australian audiences by storm.

The English ballerina, Ann Jenner, centre, in the title role in The Australian Ballet's 1980 production of Raymonda. The choreography was by Rudolf Nureyev, after Petipa, and reproduced by Marilyn Jones. Raymonda is danced to music by Glazounov.

appearance as Marguerite de Valois, Queen of France, the young Australian tenor, Anson Austin emerged as the hero of the night, although not everyone was pleased. 'The Australian Opera gave its first performance ever of Meyerbeer's four-hour blockbuster, Les Huguenots, at the Opera House on Friday night,' wrote Maria Prerauer. 'Why? There must be easier ways of boring an audience. Cheaper too.'

Joan Sutherland seemed to thoroughly enjoy the chance to kick up her heels when she appeared as flighty Rosalinde in Johann Strauss's Die Fledermaus, the 'smash hit' of 1982. One of the season's performances of this effervescent operetta became the first production televised from the Opera Theatre around Australia.

In 1983 everyone expected that 'the concert of the century', starring La Stupenda and Luciano Pavarotti, would be the triumph of the season — or the performances in the Opera Theatre of La Bohême, starring Pavarotti as Rodolfo and his lovely young protégée, the American soprano, Madelyn Renee, as Mimi. Yet within a few days of

those performances came news of the 'truly magical' premiere of Gounod's Roméo et Juliette. The opera was produced in the Concert Hall by Sir Robert Helpmann, with the beautiful, red-haired Australian soprano, Glenys Fowles, and Anson — 'handsome' — Austin in the title roles.

As they say, 'Come to the opera and enjoy love, sex, adultery, lust, murder, jealousy, insanity, revenge, greed and more . . .' Life has not been without its moments of high tension behind the scenes either. Backstage dramas have sometimes threatened to rival any presented on stage. Conflicts about repertoire, casting and other matters have resulted in The Australian Opera having three general managers since it moved into the Opera House ten years ago: The Dane, John Winther, the Englishman, Peter Hemmings, and the American, Patrick Veitch. Mr Veitch is a former member of the staff of the Metropolitan Opera, New York. He has been The Australian Opera's vigorous chief executive since 1980.

When The Australian Ballet is in residence at the Opera House, 'class' takes place every day except Sunday. There is a morning class before rehearsals and another class before the evening performance. Every dancer in the company, including the ballerinas and the premier danseurs, religiously takes daily class. Opera House staff, anxious to acquire the strong, supple figure of a dancer, have been known to seek permission to join the evening classes. No one has ever been refused, but after outfitting themselves with tights, leotards, leg-warmers, head-bands and ballet slippers, employees have quickly discovered that ballet exercises are not as effortless as they appear. Yet the dancers emerge from their gruelling practices of spinning, leaping and catapulting across the studio looking little the worse for wear; and as they jauntily make their way to the Green Room canteen for their salads and fruit drinks, their lithe figures are often the subject of envy. The willowy corphées and regal ballerinas can look as enchanting in their practice clothes as they do on stage in tiaras and tutus. Canteen staff always say that dancers are more conscious of their diets than singers, although it is surprising to find that many dancers smoke. Singers, of course, ever conscious of 'the voice' and desperately afraid of sore throats, are inclined to flee at the sight of a cigarette. The famous American mezzo-soprano, Marilyn Horne, who was an Australian Broadcasting Commission guest artist in 1978, even asked smoking journalists to leave her Sydney press conference.

A former artistic director of The Australian Ballet, Anne Woolliams, who is now Dean of Dance at the Victorian College of the Arts, highly recommends ballet for health and fitness. 'I wish more Australian parents would have their boys taught ballet,' she said. 'It doesn't matter if they are not gifted. They will develop strong, athletic bodies just the same.'

The ballerina, Marilyn Jones. In 1982 she ended a 20-year career with The Australian Ballet as artistic director of the company.

Left. Raymond Myers as Verdi's Rigoletto and Joan Carden as Gilda — Opera Theatre, 1980.

Anne Woolliams, Dean of Dance at the Victorian College of the Arts, is a former artistic director of The Australian Ballet, and first toured with the Stuttgart Ballet in 1974.

Far left. The coronation scene from Mussorgsky's epic, Boris Godunov, with the Australian bass, Donald Shanks, as the guilt-stricken tsar — Opera Theatre, 1980. Above left. Kelvin Coe and Lynette Mann — pas de deux from Nutcracker. Centre. David Burch, Janne Blanch and Dale Barker in Threshold. Above. Kelvin Coe and Lynette Mann in The Three Musketeers by Andre Prokovsky, with music by Verdi arranged by Guy Woolfenden. The ballet was presented in the Opera Theatre by the Australian Ballet in 1980. Left. Michela Kirkaldie and Peter Imbesi in The Australian Ballet's production of The Three Musketeers — Opera Theatre, 1980.

Above left. April Ward as Olga and Paul de Masson as Lensky in John Cranko's Onegin presented in 1981. The production, reproduced by Anne Woolliams, was first performed at the Opera House by The Australian Ballet in 1976. Above. The Russian-born dancers Valentina and Leonid Koslov in a new version of Afternoon Of A Faun by Jerome Robbins, to the music of Debussy, presented by The Australian Ballet in 1981. Right. David Burch, Joanne Michel and David Palmer in Variaciones Concertantes by Choo San Goh, with music by Alberto Ginastera. Left. Dale Baker, Terese Power and Paul de Masson of The Australian Ballet in Kettentanz by Gerald Arpino, with music by Johann Strauss Senior. It was presented as part of a Triple Bill in 1980.

Yet even the most gifted dancers find that the ballet offers a relatively short career. The opera coach, Jack Metz, has said that singers, properly trained, 'do not begin to enter their golden years until they are in their forties,' but that is the time of life when most dancers retire from the stage. 'The audience wants to see you do your double whammies,' said one of Australia's most distinguished dancers, Kelvin Coe, during an interview. 'No matter how hard you work at it, you can't do your double whammies when you're over forty,' he said. Coe, thirty-seven, and still very much in demand, was asked if he might be tempted to continue his career after forty. Several other famous dancers actually have. 'I wouldn't do it to the audience,' he said. 'I think the saddest thing in theatre is a disappointed audience.' He added that most dancers plan a second career after forty. It may be teaching or directing. Directing, however, seems almost as exhausting as dancing. A rehearsal makes that clear. 'Again!' The Australian Ballet's artistic director, Maina Gielgud, will order. 'No!' she will interrupt and leave her seat in the theatre to go onstage to tilt heads, twist errant torsos, mould wayward arms and legs or dance a few steps herself, to demonstrate exactly how the choreography should be interpreted. She will go back to

Leona Mitchell in the title role in Puccini's Manon Lescaut — 1980. The opera is based on the tale by the Abbe Provost.

Left. Michela Kirkaldie and Kelvin Coe in Scheherazade by Fokine, with music by Rimsky-Korsakov, presented by The Australian Ballet in 1980.

Jack Metz, opera coach to many an established and aspiring singer, believes his proteges enter their 'golden years' in their forties.

Dame Peggy van Praagh, foundation artistic director of The Australian Ballet, originally came to Australia to direct the Borovansky Company.

her seat or remain onstage as the 'piano rehearsal' continues, but only, it seems, for a few seconds, before interjecting with advice once more. Yet despite the endless interruptions, which must be extremely taxing for all concerned, displays of temperament are rare. Everyone seems totally dedicated and determined to 'get it right', even if it takes all night.

The Australian Ballet was formed in 1962 by the Australian Elizabethan Theatre Trust, assisted by J. C. Williamson's Pty. Ltd. Some of the foundation members of the company, including Kathleen Gorham, Peggy Sager and Garth Welch, began their careers as dancers with the Borovansky Ballet, one of Australia's first ballet companies. It was founded by the Czechoslovakian dancer and choreographer, Edouard Borovansky. He first visited Australia in the 1920's, as a member of Anna Pavlova's touring company. He returned in 1939 as a member of the De Basil Ballet Russe de Monte Carlo. World War II broke out during that tour and members of the company, like the touring Vienna Boys' Choir, were stranded in Australia. In 1940 Borovansky and his wife, Xenia, who was also a dancer with the De Basil Company, opened a ballet school in Melbourne and in 1942 Borovansky formed a company with the young Australians he had been teaching and some of the dancers of the then scattered De Basil company. Administered by J. C. Williamson's Theatres, the Borovansky company performed around Australia until 1957, when Borovansky died during a season at Her Majesty's Theatre in Sydney. The English dance director, Peggy van Praagh, was hurriedly brought out from England to supervise the remaining performances. The company and the Borovansky school were disbanded in 1961. Then with no other opportunities for a ballet career in Australia, many of the company's dancers left to seek employment overseas.

Above. Lynette Mann as Valencienne and Gary Norman as Danilo in Franz Lehar's The Merry Widow, 1981. Robert Helpmann's balletic version of the operetta was first presented in 1975. Right. Bruce Martin, Beryl Furlan, Marilyn Zschau and John Pringle in Meyerbeer's Les Huguenots. Left. Joan Carden and Margreta Elkins in Robert Helpmann's production of Handel's little performed opera, Alcina in 1981. Far left. Catherine Duval and Lamberto Fulan in John Copley's production of Puccini's Tosca.

Left. Valentina and Leonid Koslov in Le Corsair presented in the Opera Theatre in 1982. Right. Paul de Masson as the Hunchback in The Australian Ballet's production of The Hunchback of Notre Dame. The ballet features choreography by Bruce Wells and music by Bartók. It was premiered in 1982. Far right. The Russian-born ballerina, Valentina Koslova, as Clara in a new version of the Nutcracker which she produced for The Australian Ballet in partnership with her husband, Leonid Koslov in 1982. Below. Dale Baker as Senor Midas in The Lady and The Fool by John Cranko, produced for The Australian Ballet by Ray Powell, with music by Verdi arranged by Charles Mackerras. Performed in 1982.

Borovansky's pioneering work included the presentation of the first distinctively Australian ballet, Terra Australis, premiered in 1946. Based on a story by Tom Rothfield, with a score commissioned from Esther Rofe, the ballet is about a beautiful maiden, Australia, seduced from her Aboriginal lover by a European explorer.

Despite success overseas, most of the expatriate dancers who began their careers with Borovansky's company agreed to return to Australia when The Australian Ballet was formed in 1962; and Peggy van Praagh, who had returned to England, was recruited back to Australia as the company's first artistic director. In 1970 she was created a Dame of the British Empire for her services to dance in Australia. She was succeeded as artistic director by Sir Robert Helpmann in 1974. Sir Robert, however, had worked with her as a co-director from 1965. In 1979 Marilyn Jones, who began her career with Borovansky and who was one of the Australian ballerinas who returned from overseas to join The Australian Ballet when it was formed, succeeded Anne Woolliams as artistic director. Marilyn Jones, internationally regarded as one of the best dancers Australia has ever produced, was awarded the Order of the British Empire for services to ballet in 1972. Her fans were saddened when her twenty-year association with The Australian Ballet ended with her resignation as artistic director in 1982. Earlier, in 1981, a strike by the company's dancers about lack of rehearsal time, which caused the cancellation of Opera House performances, led to the resignation from the company of another particular favourite of audiences, the premier danseur, Kelvin Coe. He has since appeared with the Sydney Dance Company. He was also featured with the ballerina, Lois Strike, in Australian Opera performances of Die Fledermaus in 1982 and 1983.

Poster for The Australian Opera's 1983 Concert Hall performances of Gounod's Romeo et Juliette, produced by Helpmann, with Anson Austin and Glenys Fowles in the title roles.

Maina Gielgud, the present artistic director of The Australian Ballet, comes from a distinguished theatrical family.

Left. Jennifer Bermingham and Leona Mitchell in John Copley's production of Puccini's Madame Butterfly.

Spartacus, one of the most popular works in the Australian Ballet's repertoire, was re-presented in 1983.

The ballerina, Maina Gielgud, of the famous theatrical family, recently retired from the stage to become The Australian Ballet's fifth artistic director. She took up the appointment in January, 1983. The company, which will celebrate its twenty-first anniversary in 1983, gave its first performance at Her Majesty's Theatre in Sydney on November 2, 1962. The inaugural season began with a production of Swan Lake.

The Australian Ballet's first Opera House season began on December 7, 1973 with a performance of The Sleeping Beauty produced by Sir Robert Helpmann, with choreography by Dame Peggy van Praagh. The New Zealand-born ballerina, Lucette Aldous, danced the title role. The company has performed regularly in the Opera Theatre since the opening season. Since 1982 it has also presented ballets in the Concert Hall. Its repertoire, while basically classical, also features contemporary works. They include The Melbourne Cup, a ballet by Helpmann, inspired by the scene at Flemington Race Course during Australia's most famous annual horse race. Beyond Twelve, a ballet about a boy's discovery of the joy of dance, was commissioned by the company from the artistic director of the contemporary Sydney Dance Company, Graeme Murphy, in 1981.

In 1975 The Australian Ballet presented the world premiere of The Merry Widow, a ballet based on Lehar's famous operetta. Produced by Sir Robert Helpmann, it was set to music from the operetta, arranged by the Australian conductor, John Lanchbery. The extravaganza, which

Above. Luciano Pavarotti as Rodolfo, Madelyn Renee as Mimi and Rhonda Bruce as Musetta in John Copley's production of Puccini's La Boheme — Opera Theatre, 1983. Left. Glenys Fowles and Anson Austin in Robert Helpmann's 1983 Concert Hall production of Romeo et Juliette by Gounod.

includes a nightclub scene during which the corps de ballet dance the can-can, was re-presented in 1981 and remains one of the most popular productions the company has ever presented.

The company tours nationally and internationally. To date it has undertaken twelve major overseas tours. Guest artists are regularly engaged — Dame Margot Fonteyn and Rudolf Nureyev are among the stars who have appeared with the company. Most productions, however, star resident principals. The majority of the present members of the company are graduates of The Australian Ballet's school, which was formed in 1964 and is based, like the company, in Melbourne. Dame Margaret Scott has been director of the school since its establishment.

Drama in the Opera Theatre has included performances of Molière's comedy, The Imaginary Invalid, which was presented in 1974 by the Stratford National Theatre of Canada. Other visiting ensembles which have appeared in the theatre include The Stuttgart Ballet, the Polish Mime Ballet Theatre and the Merce Cunningham Dance Company of New York. Performances of Death to the Bogeyman by La Claca, the avant garde theatre group of Catalonia, astounded many members of the audience in 1980, but the season was enthusiastically applauded by the critics. The production, described in advertisements as 'a brilliant carnival of mime and dance with giant puppets designed by Joan Miró, included a scene which featured a cowering sycophant attempting to ingratiate himself with a constipated tyrant by applauding the overload as he defaecated.

The Radio Symphony Orchestra of Saarbrücken, the Sofia Soloists and the Jean-Francois Paillard Orchestra are among the orchestras which have performed in the Opera Theatre.

The visit of the Russian ballet stars Mikhail Barishnikov and Natalia Makarova in 1974 was looked forward to as eagerly as that of Pavarotti in 1983. The dancers were engaged for a season with Ballet Victoria by the Australian entrepreneur, Michael Edgley. Barishnikov, however, injured his ankle on the first night and was forced to leave the stage and cancel all of his remaining Australian performances. Rarely has there been such disappointment at the Opera House. The Australian dancer, Garth Welch, who had retired from the stage, made an heroic return when he stepped in at less than twenty-four hours notice to replace Barishnikov, partner Makarova and save the season. The programme presented included Giselle Act Three and Divertissements.

Dame Margot Fonteyn was an early visitor to the Opera House and has excited Australian balletomanes on a number of memorable occasions.

Dame Margaret Scott, founder-director of The Australian Ballet School which began training young dancers in 1964, is still in control.

THE PLAY'S THE THING

The Drama Theatre

An illustration by T.L. Madrazo featured on the programme for The Old Tote Theatre Company's opening season production of The Threepenny Opera by Bertold Brecht.

Thousands of American servicemen spent time in Australia during World War II, when the Japanese were menacing the country. "Over-sexed, over-paid and over here" was a wartime expression which summed up the nature of the supposed threat posed by the visitors. Australian servicemen sorely resented the attentions these Americans paid their womenfolk — and especially the rapture with which those attentions were often received. The Allied authorities have since been accused of suppressing news of pitched battles which broke out over the favours of Australian women. But Bob Herbert's play, No Names No Pack Drill, is not an exposé of the measures taken by the military chiefs to conceal the fact that their forces were sometimes more intent on attacking each other than the Japanese. Even though the play hints at the resentment, bewilderment and broken hearts which were the legacy of many Australian-American wartime liaisons, it is a comedy which evokes the frantic pace of life in Sydney in 1942 as servicemen and civilians attempted to enjoy, or profit or escape from their war. Mel Gibson, who has since become internationally known through appearances in such films as Gallipoli and the Mad Max series, played the part of Rebel Potter — a Purple Heart winner, wounded at Guadalcanal, who cannot face the battlefield again. Noni Hazlehurst was Kathy McLeod, the post office mail sorter with a husband away fighting in New Guinea, who tries to help Potter escape to the United States on a freighter. The supporting characters include an Australian blackmarketeer, a determinedly pragmatic American corporal, his compliant, giggling girlfriend, and an acute, spiteful landlady.

It was one of the most successful productions of the 1980 season. As is invariably the case in Australia the play had no "running in" period. The lack of experimental theatres in the cities, and the shortage of provincial theatres has prevented Australian companies from following the overseas practice of "trying out" new shows "out of town". The cost of touring around the vast continent is another difficulty.

Roy Dotrice as John Aubrey in Brief Lives, Drama Theatre 1975. It was an individual performance of great distinction and the make-up preparation took many patient hours.

Left. Robin Ramsay as Macheath and Pamela Stephenson as Polly Peachum in The Old Tote Theatre Company's opening season production of The Threepenny Opera by Bertold Brecht.

Machinery below the Drama Theatre stage, used to operate the 'revolve' which makes scene changes swiftly and magically above.

Noni Hazlehurst, as Kathy McLeod, Ron Falk as Detective Sergeant Browning and Mel Gibson as Rebel Potter in Bob Herbert's No Names No Pack Drill. The play was directed by George Ogilvie, with sets by Kristian Fredrikson and costumes by Anna French.

Originally it was intended that Opera House productions of drama and musical comedy would be presented in the second-largest theatre, but because of the interior design changes made in 1967, that theatre became the Opera Theatre, and the area Utzon had set aside for experimental theatre became the principal venue for drama.

Unlike the Concert Hall and the Opera Theatre, the Drama Theatre is not crowned with a set of soaring sails, and the theatregoer does not mount a monumental staircase to reach the auditorium. The theatre's entrance is at ground level, on the Opera House promenade, facing the Harbour Bridge and the International Shipping Terminal. If the weather is fine, it is on the promenade rather than in the theatre's foyer that most patrons enjoy their drinks at interval; and matinee audiences can often be seen milling about in the sunshine between the acts of a play.

The Drama Theatre features John Coburn's vivid tapestry Curtain of the Moon, and seats five hundred and forty four. All the seats give an excellent view of the stage, the acoustics are resonant, but the theatre's design creates technical problems. The stage is very wide — twenty-one metres — and achieving an intimate atmosphere is difficult. The theatre also has poor access for scenery. Neither the backstage nor front-of-house entrances are big enough to allow large pieces of scenery to be carried in whole. They must be designed in sections and built up on stage. With a total stage depth of sixteen metres, however, and a rear

Curtain of the Moon, a striking feature of the Drama Theatre, was woven from Australian wool by the tapestry-making firm of Pinton Frères, near Aubusson in France. The curtain is nine metres high and 16 metres wide. Its abstract shapes represent plant forms.

stage area four metres deep, eighteen metres wide and eight metres high, it is possible to accommodate several sets for scene changes behind the backdrop. Wing space is miniscule. The wings are reached by a spiral staircase leading from a corridor which gives access to the theatre's dressing rooms. The corridor also serves as a passageway to many of the Opera House's administration offices. Office staff have learnt to be considerate of the actors and actresses often seen pacing the corridor awaiting their cues to descend to the wings. New employees are cautioned not to interrupt the cast or even compliment them on their costumes. On one occasion in March, 1974 the management was embarrassed when the squeals of startled office girls distracted the Aboriginal actor, Jack Charles, who had to make an entrance naked and walked from his dressing room, en route to the stage, in front of the girls. He was appearing as Bennelong in Michael Boddy's play, The Cradle of Hercules. The cast also included the distinguished Australian actor, John Gaden, as the well-intentioned but paternalistic Governor Arthur Phillip. The argument of the play is that time has stood still in European attitudes about Aborigines.

Such serious drama is commonly on the Drama Theatre pro-gramme but light entertainment is also presented; the theatre's fore-stage can be lowered and used as an orchestral pit accommodating up to thirty musicians. It is electrically powered and also serves as a transport lift to a storage area beneath the stage.

Above. Heather Mitchell, Tyler Coppin, Jane Harders and Tim McKenzie in You Can't Take It With You. Above right. Judy Davis as Lulu. The State Theatre Company of South Australia's production of this tragedy was presented as part of the 1981 season. Opposite page. John Bell as Cyrano in the Sydney Theatre Company's production of Cyrano de Bergerac. Bottom right. Chincilla, a play about Diaghilev, Nijinsky and Massine was presented in 1981. The cast was headed by Peter Carroll as Diaghilev. Right. Noni Hazlehurst as Miss Clemmy Hummer in The Man From Mukinupin.

The musical, Chicago, was the smash hit of the 1981 Drama Theatre season with the Australian, Nancy Hayes, starring as the razzle-dazzler, Roxy, who gets away with murder! After six weeks of capacity houses, the cast left the Opera House in costume, bound for a second season at Sydney's Theatre Royal. Their procession through the city's streets in a fleet of vintage cars was led by a Dixieland jazz band playing on a flat-top truck streamered with banners proclaiming that "Roxy's now rocking at de Royal".

Many Drama Theatre productions, including Bob Herbert's No Names No Pack Drill, have had second seasons at other Sydney theatres following premieres at the Opera House. Because the schedule for all the theatres is decided at least a year in advance, one production immediately follows another, and no season can be extended, no matter

A scene from the song and dance show, An Evening, first presented by the Sydney Dance Company in 1981. An Evening was produced by Graeme Murphy and Kristian Fredrickson and starred the Australian singer, Geraldine Turner.

how overwhelming the demand. Although entrepreneurs prefer to take advantage of an Opera House success by immediately transferring the production to another Sydney theatre, highly successful Opera House productions are often presented again as soon as practicable. Edmond Rostand's Cyrano de Bergerac, with the Australian actor, John Bell, giving a distinguished performance as Cyrano was re-presented in the Opera Theatre in 1981 following a capacity season in the Drama Theatre in 1980.

While Australian audiences have not yet shown much enthusiasm for Australian operas like Rites of Passage or Lenz, they receive Australian plays well, especially those which mirror their own experience like David Williamson's What If You Died Tomorrow? A great success in the 1973 season, it was preceded by productions of Shakespeare's Richard II and Bertolt Brecht and Kurt Weill's The Threepenny Opera, which attracted only moderate interest. David Williamson is concerned with contemporary life in middle-income Australia and his satire, What If You Died Tomorrow? is about an evening at home with a young man who has just become a successful novelist after having left his wife and two children. He is living now in an artists' colony with his journalist girlfriend and her three children. His publisher, his agent and his parents all call during the evening of the play. His parents' sex life is among the subjects he examines with merciless scrutiny.

Another of Williamson's plays, The Perfectionist, is a comedy about a self-important academic with a wife who feels that her own talents have for too long been sacrificed to her husband's interests. It was the decided success of the 1982 season.

While most of the characters in David Williamson's plays are prepared to discuss the most intimate and indelicate details of their lives, John Powell's The Last of the Knucklemen is about a dying breed — the reticent male of Australian folklore, with a preference for settling disputes with his fists and a Ned Kelly tendency to 'shoot through' — run away from the law, his wife, his debts — or any other problem defying immediate resolution. The Last of the Knucklemen is set in 1973 in a mining camp in the north — an area then so desperate for labour that a man's antecedents or immediate past were not investigated too closely. The play, produced by the Melbourne Theatre Company, was presented in the Drama Theatre in 1974 by the Australian Elizabethan Theatre Trust. The Old Tote Theatre Company, however, presented most Drama Theatre programmes from 1973 until 1978, when the company was disbanded because of financial and administrative problems.

The Old Tote had been founded by the Australian Elizabethan Theatre Trust in 1963 and became self-governing about six years later. The company was established in the grounds of the University of New

A Doll's House by Ibsen was presented as part of the 1976 Drama Theatre season.

Programme design by Shane Porteous for The Old Tote Theatre Company's first production in the Drama Theatre of Shakespeare's tragic King Richard the Second.

South Wales in the Sydney suburb of Kensington. The grounds were once the site of a racecourse and the company took its name from an old totalizator building which was converted for use as its first theatre, workshop and office. In its heyday the company frequently presented productions simultaneously at Kensington, the Opera House and other Sydney theatres. It received financial support from both the Australian and New South Wales Governments and until its sudden closure it was the principal drama group in New South Wales.

The Old Tote's Opera House seasons continually attracted scathing criticism, but there were acknowledged successes as well as failures. The company presented a total of forty-one productions and fifteen hundred performances in the Drama Theatre between 1973 and 1978. Its greatest success was its 1977 production of Maxim Gorky's harrowing play, The Lower Depths, directed by the Romanian, Liviu Ciulei. Earlier successes included the 1975 one-man show, Brief Lives, with the English actor, Roy Dotrice, unforgettable as the wily old gossip, John Aubrey, hobbling about his filthy lodgings in Dirty Lane, Bloomsbury in 1697 — the last year of his life — chucking slops out the window and treating audiences to a succession of penetrating observations and bawdy anecdotes about the intrigue and scandal of the day.

1976, however, was a heyday year for The Tote. Its Opera House season offered a magnificently haunting production of Tennessee Williams' A Streetcar Named Desire, directed by Richard Wherrett, and with one of the country's most distinguished actresses, Robyn Nevin, as Blanche Dubois; Eugene O'Neill's tragedy, Mourning Becomes Electra, directed by Bill Redmond, which also starred Robyn Nevin, and The Season at Sarsaparilla, a play by Australia's Nobel laureate, Patrick White, directed by Jim Sharman.

The Season at Sarsaparilla is about life in the sprawling poorer suburbs of Australia in the late 1950's. It is summertime, hot and humid, and there are no indoor lavatories. The audience is invited into three households to be devastated by the dreary routine of daily life. The heads of the households: a perky men's wear salesman, a pompous, small-time business executive and a stoical sanitary carter — the untouchable of the street — leave for work. Their listless wives stay home to read advertisements for manchester and new appliances and snap at the children and the dogs "on heat". Working wives were a rarity in Australia in the 1950's, even in the poorer suburbs. The only heroine to emerge is Nola Boyle, the wife of the sanitary carter who realizes that life must have adventure and excitement — if only episodically. She risks the censure of her world when she seeks momentary fulfilment in the marital bed with her husband's virile mate, Digger Masson. Although The Season at Sarsaparilla was enjoyed by Opera House audiences, the play infuriated many Australians when it was first

The playwright, David Williamson, pictured here in 1973, portrays contemporary Australian life with analytic zeal and a fine wit.

Patrick White, Australia's sole Nobel Prizewinner for Literature. His novels, short stories and plays examine the Australian experience, sometimes with prophetic edge.

Scene from Patrick White's The Season at Sarsaparilla, presented by The Old Tote in 1976. Directed by Jim Sharman and designed by Wendy Dickson, the cast included Kate Fitzpatrick, Paul Bertram, Michele Fawdon, Peter Whitford, Robyn Nevin, Max Cullen and Bill Hunter.

produced in Adelaide in 1962 and probably more accurately mirrored the attitudes and way of life of thousands of suburbanites.

The Old Tote's repertoire also included a play by another Australian playwright, Dorothy Hewett's Chapel Perilous. It was an early work, the story of a resilient Australian country girl, exceptionally hungry for the joys and challenges of life. The play was not a great success but Hewett was to achieve fame at the Opera House in 1981, when the Sydney Theatre Company broke all the existing attendance records for the theatre with its production of her comedy, The Man From Mukinupin.

This comedy, described by the The Sydney Morning Herald's theatre critic, H. G. Kippax, as "not quite a comedy, but certainly a comedy with music" — by Jim Cotter — is set between 1912 and 1920 in an arid wheatbelt township in Western Australia. Perhaps the highlight was an astonishing performance of the Death of Desdemona by two travelling actors, played by Ruth Cracknell and John Gaden.

Above left. Nina Veretennikova — in red — and other members of the Sydney Dance Company in LM514, by Graeme Watson. Far left. Anna-Maria Winchester and Kenneth Laird in Chekhov's Ivanov. Left. Gillian Jones, Robyn Nevin, Andrew Tighe and Ned Manning in The Precious Woman by Louis Nowra. Above. John Hargreaves as Brick and Wendy Hughes as Maggie in Tennessee Williams' Cat On A Hot Tin Roof. Far right. Shane Porteous and Kirrily Nolan in David Williamson's What If You Died Tomorrow? Right. Peter Carroll and Robyn Nevin as the married couple in David Williamson's The Perfectionist.

The Sydney Theatre Company was established by the New South Wales Premier, Mr Neville Wran, in 1978. The company was formed, virtually overnight, to replace The Old Tote. The Old Tote's final season in the Drama Theatre ended on December 12 that year with a performance of the French farce, The Lady From Maxim's by Georges Feydeau. The Sydney Theatre Company's first annual season in the theatre began a little over a month later with a production of Patrick White's The Cheery Soul. The play tells the story of Miss Docker, an ageing, wiry spinster whose craving for consolation and a more impressive identity leads her to drive her aquaintances to distraction with relentless attention and enquiries.

The Sydney Theatre Company was able to arrange a 1979 'interim' season of world drama at the Opera House with incredible speed because five other Sydney and suburban companies rallied to its aid, each of them contributing a production to this season. In fact, the short-lived Paris Company contributed two plays to this highly successful first season: The Lady of the Camellias, by Dumas, with Kate Fitzpatrick in the title role, and Patrick White's The Cheery Soul with Robyn Nevin as Miss Docker. The 1979 programme also included Bernard Shaw's The Devil's Disciple, produced by the Q Theatre of Penrith, Eugene O'Neill's Long Day's Journey into Night, produced by the Ensemble Theatre of North Sydney, Bertold Brecht's The Caucasian Chalk Circle, contributed by the NIDA/Jane Street Company, and a particularly popular production of Carlo Goldoni's The Venetian Twins, directed by John Bell of Sydney's Nimrod Theatre, with Drew Forsythe giving a virtuoso performance in the dual role of the twin brothers.

The Way of the World, presented by the Sydney Theatre Company in 1983, was dressed stylishly in Restoration costume.

The stage settings for Congreve's Way of the World were as contemporary as 1983 but the gowns were pure eighteenth century.

Left. Tony Phillips and other members of the Sydney Theatre Company's Wardrobe Department at work. Currently sharing space with the Elizabethan Theatre Trust, the company hopes for a home of its own in a renovated warehouse on Sydney Harbour, near the Opera House.

In the meantime, the Sydney Theatre Company had engaged the highly regarded Australian director, Richard Wherrett, as its artistic director and had been busy planning subsequent seasons. Most of the companies which perform at the Opera House have a resident complement of artists, but the Sydney Theatre Company has followed The Old Tote's practice of operating with a resident production and administrative team and engaging actors, guest directors and designers on a production by production basis. The company has also followed The Old Tote's practice of presenting a programme of six plays in the Drama Theatre each year, each scheduled for a run of about six to seven weeks.

While most of the ensembles which contributed to the company's first 'interim' season in the Drama Theatre have since been stricken with financial problems that have threatened their existence — sadly The Paris Company has actually gone out of business — the Sydney Theatre Company has firmly established itself as one of Australia's leading drama groups.

The company's first independent season at the Opera House began in January, 1980 with a summer holiday production of the Anglo-Australian melodrama, The Sunny South. Written in the 19th century by George Darrell, the play is about an indestructible young Englishman who battles on the Australian goldfields to win a fortune and save his genteel family from bankruptcy. Before the curtain went up on the first night the Australian actress, Ruth Cracknell, read a prologue especially written for the occasion by playwright, David Williamson:

The design of a costume worn by Pamela Stephenson as Queen Isabel in The Old Tote Theatre production of Richard II.

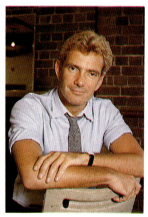

Richard Wherrett has been artistic director of the Sydney Theatre Company since its formation in 1978. Appointed after a long experience with the Nimrod Theatre, he has shown imaginative flair in the development of the company.

Oh Opera House, oh hulking beast,
Whose sail doth rise like dough with yeast,
Tonight you spawn within your belly,
A living rival to the telly.
Wherret's mob or Sydney's folly.
Call them what you will, by golly.
They're poised at edge of this decade
All pledged to serve a cavalcade
Of theatre grand and wise and soaring,
Passionate, vulgar, never boring.
And if they do half of that,
I swear by good Greg Chappell's bat
That Sydney will be far the richer,

A mirror held to life's great pitcher.
And if perchance, the odd show stinks,
At interval, there's always drinks,
The harbour bridge, ships on the move,
Second act may well improve.
So, onward now into the 80's,
And crucial years they will be, maties.
The world can boast no finer city,
But scenic beauty, more's the pity,
Cannot give the depth of soul,
Without the arts, no city's whole.
And now I'll shut my great big mouth
And let you see The Sunny South.

Like most of the national and state companies which perform at the Opera House the Sydney Theatre Company is associated with the Opera House's daytime series of budget-priced introductory programmes, designed to introduce people of all ages to opera, ballet, drama and music. The programmes feature an act from an opera, a play or ballet, or part of a concert programme, followed or preceded by a talk, given by a director, conductor or dancer about the behind-the-scenes preparations for the performance.

The Sydney Theatre Company's policy is to include new Australian plays, as well as dramas and comedies from the international repertoire in all its seasons. Louis Nowra's The Precious Woman, John O'Donohue's A Happy and Holy Occasion, Bob Herbert's No Names No Pack Drill, David Williamson's The Perfectionist and Dorothy Hewett's The Man From Mukinupin and The Fields of Heaven — a play about the conflict between new European settlers and established Australian landowners — are among the Australian plays the company has presented. Its 1983 season included Gossip From The Forest, one of the few Australian plays with a European scenario. Set in France and based on Thomas Keneally's novel of the same name, its subject is the merciless terms of the peace treaty which brought World War 1 to an end.

Ron Haddrick as Tom Barrow, Sally McKenzie as Lucia Silvieri and Lex Marinos as Rome Bodera in a scene from Dorothy Hewett's The Fields of Heaven.

Right. The courtroom scene from The Marionette Theatre of Australia's rod-puppet production of The Magic Pudding.

The Magic Pudding, written and illustrated by Norman Lindsay and first published in 1918, is the best known Australian fairy story. The Marionette Theatre's faithful adaptation of the book has frequently been a popular school holiday attraction.

The artistic director of the Marionette Theatre of Australia, Richard Bradshaw, emerging from rehearsal. The puppets, Morton Barman and Koala Supremo, were featured in Captain Lazaar And His Earthbound Circus, produced in the Recording Hall in 1980.

The Marionette Theatre of Australia — Australia's National Puppet Theatre — and the Sydney Dance Company are two other companies which regularly perform in the Drama Theatre usually between plays presented by the Sydney Theatre Company. In fact the Marionette Theatre and the drama company often perform in the theatre simultaneously — with daytime puppet shows for children and evening drama performances for mature audiences.

The Marionette Theatre was formed in 1965 by the Australian Elizabethan Theatre Trust. The company, which performs around Australia and regularly tours overseas, became self-governing in 1980 and has since established its headquarters in an old Sailors' Home, built in the Victorian era, in Sydney's historic Rocks area. The old refuge, with its rectangular hall and galleries of tiny cabins, obviously designed with the intention of encouraging seamen to sleep alone, is currently being extensively renovated and will eventually house an indoor and outdoor theatre, workshops, administrative offices and bistros. The company plans, however, to continue its popular school holiday performances at the Opera House. Its repertoire also includes productions for adult audiences — such as Captain Lazaar and His Earthbound Circus — a satire on the political personalities and events associated with the dismissal of the Whitlam Government in 1975.

The Marionette Theatre has about twenty members, including puppet-making, production and administrative staff, and it engages guest producers, writers, puppeteers, cartoonists and musicians for individual productions. Richard Bradshaw has been the company's artistic director since its formation.

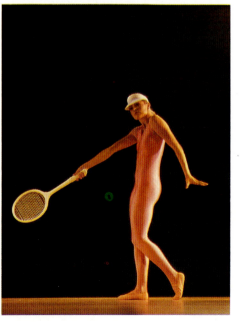

Above. A scene from the Sydney Dance Company's 1981 production of An Evening. Far left. Susan Barling in Week-day Dreaming – Part 1 of the Dance Trilogy 'Rumours'. Left. Susan Barling and Ros Philip in Bare Facts and Fantasies – part II of the trilogy Rumours by Graeme Murphy. Danced to music by the Australian composer, Barry Conyngham, it was first presented in the Drama Theatre by the Sydney Dance Company in 1972. Right. Nina Veretennikova and Robert Olup in Rumours, Part I. The three-part ballet is about hedonistic life in Sydney and growing old and dependent on others for survival.

The Sydney Dance Company has accomplished a feat which most arts administrators thought impossible. It has created an enthusiastic following for contemporary dance in Australia. A decade ago there was the same lack of interest in contemporary dance as there is in contemporary opera today. Yet the young Dance Company, like the tough kid down the street, persisted, despite the hard knocks. In fact, the commitment with which its dancers prepared for performances, while realizing that there was little interest in their programmes at the box office and that they might be disbanded at any moment because of lack of money, has even been described as heroic.

Ron Haddrick and Dinah Shearing in the opening season production of Richard II.

Scene from The Old Tote's 1974 production of Shakespeare's Macbeth in the Opera Theatre. Ron Haddrick appeared in the title role and Dinah Shearing played Lady Macbeth. The Sydney Theatre Company presented a new production of the play in 1982, when John Bell appeared in the title role.

Despite the Opera House's magnetism, the company's early performances in the Concert Hall and the Opera Theatre attracted embarrassingly small houses. Rather than have her dancers confronted by row after row of empty seats, the company's founder, Sue Musitz, would ask the box office to "paper the house": attract a larger audience by dispensing free seats. The dance critics, however, were consistently encouraging — often finding the company's innovative choreography and starkly effective costumes and sets more "relevant" than the opulent productions of the classically based national company, The Australian Ballet.

Mainly because of the favourable press reports, audiences, especially younger audiences, gradually began to take notice of the daring, younger company which often danced to taped music by rock and pop groups and which was able to express the experiences and yearnings of the young through dance. Within a few years the ensemble was not only attracting capacity houses but touring nationally and internationally.

Financial problems, however, continue to beset the company. Its founder, Sue Musitz had continually to race to and from rehearsals to lobby in the offices of politicians, arts administrators and businessmen for funds to pay her dancers and meet the other costs of performances. Today, mainly because of extensive touring commitments, the company's management is still finding the expense of production greater than box office receipts, despite good houses.

Sue Musitz established the company in 1971. It was known as the Dance Company (NSW) until 1978, by which time Graeme Murphy had replaced Miss Musitz as artistic director. Murphy, widely regarded as the most brilliant choreographer Australia has ever produced, has led the company through its most successful years, but Sue Musitz's work in founding the ensemble and the fight she put up to ensure that it survived its infancy is recognized as perhaps the most significant contribution to dance in Australia in recent years.

The company, which now has a complement of 20 dancers and a small administrative staff, is based on the waterfront, at Woolloomooloo, a couple of kilometres from the Opera House. It performs most frequently in the Drama Theatre but also presents occasional seasons in the Concert Hall and the Opera Theatre and at other Sydney theatres. The company appears with various orchestras and ensembles and regularly commissions work from Australian composers as well as choreographers. Its repertoire is comprised almost exclusively of Australian ballets. Rumours, a ballet about hedonistic life in contemporary Sydney, is perhaps its most popular to date. Choreographed by Graeme Murphy, with one of its scenes set at Sydney's nude bathing resort, Lady Jane Beach, it was premiered in the Drama Theatre in 1979 and has been presented several times since.

Sue Musitz established the Sydney Dance Company in 1971. Originally known as the Dance Company (NSW), it has survived many vicissitues and is a tribute to her faith and tenacity.

Graeme Murphy, artistic director of The Sydney Dance Company since 1978, is acclaimed as a brilliant choreographer and has also been employed by The Australian Ballet.

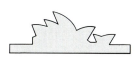

RECEPTION HALL
CONCERT HALL
OPERA THEATRE
BOX OFFICE

INFORMATION
BENNELONG
RESTAURANT
THE SHOP

EXHIBI
MUS

ONE
WAY →

THE SILVER SCREEN

The Cinema

Six of the 224 abstract pictures in crayon and fabric dyes from Sidney Nolan's Little Shark mural. The artist donated the work to the Opera House in 1973.

Left. A shot from the film, Storm Riders. The sound-track featured music by the Little River Band, Men at Work, Split Enz, Australian Crawl and was shown in the Cinema in 1982.

Guided tours of the Opera House set off from the foyer of the Cinema. A tour of the building takes an hour and staff guides lead as many as seven tours a day. 'No wonder you are in such great shape,' complimented the American television commentator, Walter Cronkite, as he accompanied a young woman guide up and down the stairs to visit all the theatres and foyers.

Young men, as well as young women, make up the building's team of a dozen permanent and casual guides. Some of the casuals are students studying for a career in the performing arts. The guides, known as the 'St Trinian's gang' by other employees, are the most popular group in the Opera House. In moments of stress it is in the guides' tiny common room that many staff seek refuge. Here there will always be commiseration and a cup of something on offer.

But the guides are admired as much for their stamina and efficiency as they are for their seemingly inexhaustible bonhomie and compassion for the underdog. 'Those poor guides,' other staff often comment, as they see one of them setting off, like Boadicea at the head of her army, on yet another tour and another round of taxing explanations — for nothing about the Opera House can be summed up simply. Quite a lengthy explanation is necessary when visitors ask why the building lacks a car park and it takes even longer to recount the history of the largest theatre, or explain the significance of some of the complex's works of art. Tours begin with a viewing of Little Shark, a mural by the Australian artist, Sir Sydney Nolan, which decorates the foyer of the cinema. The painting is a composite work, made up of two hundred and twenty-four abstract pictures in crayon and fabric dyes, executed on glossy paper. After studying this intriguing mural for a couple of minutes, most people can detect the outline of the big fish, but others remain mystified. A viewing of the painting usually ends with part of a touring party sketching sharks in the air as they help the guide to convince the rest of the group that the outline can be clearly seen. 'Stand back and study the lighter centre section,' the guide will advise. 'Light and shade play an important part.' There was not enough room to

The souvenir shop on the Concourse is currently operated by Marilyn Zweck and offers a wide variety of quality mementoes, books and pictures of the Opera House.

hang the entire work, which is about four metres high and fourteen metres wide. A section of it was transferred to the general manager's office and sixteen pictures now enliven his walls.

Among the books on sale in the Opera House shop during the opening season was a fifty-cent work which featured photographs and a brief description of the theatres. Of the second smallest theatre it said: 'The Music Room seats four hundred and twenty. This theatre will be used for chamber music, recitals, solo performances and the screening of films.' In fact, the Music Room has been used most frequently for films and was re-named the 'Cinema' in 1979.

Nonetheless Australia's leading promoter of chamber music, Musica Viva Australia, was expected to be the major hirer of this theatre. The company did present several of its opening season concerts there but transferred its subsequent seasons to the Concert Hall because of the demand for tickets. As audiences continued to grow, the company also began presenting annual seasons at Sydney's Seymour Centre which opened in 1975.

Musica Viva now presents one or two concerts a month at the Opera House between March and November. It is a national organisation operating from its Sydney headquarters with a staff of fifteen. It engages Australian and visiting quartets, trios, chamber orchestras, choirs and soloists for performances in capital cities, country towns and schools throughout Australia. It also commissions music from Australian composers and organizes overseas tours by the Australian Chamber Orchestra, the Sydney String Quartet and other leading Australian ensembles.

Musica Viva was formed in Sydney as a music society in 1945 by the Viennese musician, Richard Goldner, and other new settlers from Europe. Except for a brief period in the early 1950's the company has been continuously active. Its initial concerts were given in spacious homes in the suburbs on Sunday afternoons and Thursday evenings. For twenty-five years, from 1948, it was administered by Regina Ridge. She was plain-spoken, iron-willed and a brilliant administrator. Single-handedly she could — and often did — engage artists, book concert venues, canvass new subscribers, arrange accommodation and transport for visiting artists and cater for post-concert receptions. With a tiny budget and her legendary efficiency, she brought Musica Viva's performances out of the drawing-rooms and onto the stages of town halls and concert halls throughout Australia. She is widely regarded as the prime mover in creating significant Australian audiences for chamber music and for turning a music society into an international concert agency. In 1974, a few months after the Opera House opened, Regina Ridge joined its staff as concert manager. Sadly she died in a road accident in 1975, during a business trip to Czechoslovakia. Musica Viva

Musica Viva arranged the first official acoustic test at the Opera House in the unfinished Music Room — now called the Cinema — on October 11, 1972.

Louis Malle's six-and-a-half-hour documentary, Phantom India, screened in two parts, attracted capacity audiences.

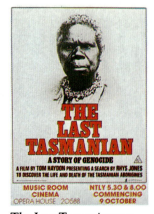

The Last Tasmanian was screened in the Cinema in the spring of 1978. It depicts the destruction of the Tasmanian Aborigines after 1803 when British colonisation began.

subscribers were among those who packed the Opera Theatre for her memorial concert and a fund set up in her memory is used to buy chamber music scores for the Opera House library.

Like Musica Viva, most of the entrepreneurs who presented performances at the Opera House during the opening season have remained faithful users of the building. The most notable exception is the Australian Film Institute. In 1982, when fees for hiring the Cinema were increased as part of a general annual price review, the Institute did not renew its option as major hirer. The news was received with disappointment. The Australian Film Institute and, earlier, the National Film Theatre of Australia — which merged in 1979 — presented screenings in the Cinema from 1973 to 1982. Their 'non-commercial' programmes included classic films, new films by young directors and co-operatives, and highly controversial films about political and social issues, such as Public Enemy Number One. This award-winning Australian documentary, directed by David Bradbury and screened in 1981, focussed on the controversial Australian journalist, Wilfred Burchett, whose world 'scoops' included the first 'on-the-spot' report of the aftermath of the atomic bomb attack on Hiroshima. But Burchett, who was born in Poowong in Victoria in 1911 and who 'jumped the rattlers' seeking work during the Great Depression, is notorious as the man accused of attempting to 'brainwash' Australian prisoners-of-war in Korea. His coverage of the Vietnam War from behind Vietcong lines also made him the subject of considerable controversy, and his seventeen-year fight to have his passport renewed by the Australian Government kept him in the news. It was restored when the Whitlam Government came to power but Burchett continues to live overseas.

First Contact, produced and directed by Bob Connolly and Robin Anderson was presented by Ronin Films in May 1983. It explores the long unknown world of the one million people living in central New Guinea.

The Goethe Institut has presented several exhibitions in association with the Sydney Opera House Trust, including an exhibition of German literature in 1981.

Alan Rich's film, Wizards of the Water, had its world premiere season at the Opera House in 1981 and a return season in 1983.

Left. Still from the Australian film, Wrong Side of the Road, directed by Ned Lander, which is about two days in the lives of the Aboriginal rock bands, No Fixed Address and Us Mob. It was screened by the Australian Film Institute in 1981.

The Sydney Harbour Bridge was officially opened on March 19, 1932. To celebrate the 50th anniversary, the Department of Main Roads mounted a display of memorabilia in the Exhibition Hall in March, 1982.

Left. An exhibition about the plays, politics and people associated with Sydney's New Theatre was on view in the Exhibition Hall in June and July 1982 to mark its 50th anniversary.

Puppets from the vast collection amassed by the Marionette Theatre of Australia were on display in the Exhibition Hall during April and May, 1979.

Not A Love Story, a Canadian documentary about pornography, directed by Bonnie Sherr Klein, was the last film presented in the Cinema by the Australian Film Institute. Ironically, this final offering, which was extensively discussed in the media, attracted record film attendances. Practically every screening in 1982 was sold out. Attendance, however, at many previous screenings had been poor, despite excellent reviews — and this was a major factor in the Institute's decision to move out and present all its future Sydney screenings at its New South Wales headquarters at Paddington Town Hall. Many people remain disappointed that the important, albeit controversial and 'non-commercial' films and documentaries exhibited by the Institute will no longer be seen at Australia's leading performing arts centre.

What attracts the crowds is surfing films with soundtracks featuring top rock groups. They have always attracted good audiences of young people and brought new life to the Opera House. The sight of them making their way along the promenade to the Cinema in their jeans, shorts and tee shirts bearing irreverent slogans has probably done more than any publicity brochure to dispel fears that the Opera House would become a centre only for a privileged few.

Holidays bring an even younger audience — and memories of the joys of being out of school and off to town to the pictures. Hundreds of children fill the Cinema for the daytime school holiday films. The promoters of these features have delighted parents because the films exhibited are genuinely suitable. As well as classics like Pinocchio and new films like Across The Great Divide, the story of two resilient orphans, stranded in the Rocky Mountains on the death of their grandfather, the school holiday programmes have included films for those thinking of a career in the performing arts. One documentary treated of children training for ballet at the Russian Kirov School.

Opera and ballet films and seasons of classic films are regularly presented for mature audiences by various entrepreneurs, including the Sydney Opera House Trust but since the departure of the Australian Film Institute, the Trust has been investigating the possibility of using the Cinema as a second venue for drama, although this plan does not preclude its use for films and other types of performances.

The Cinema, like the Drama Theatre, lies at ground level. Its entrance is on the promenade facing the Harbour Bridge and the International Shipping Terminal. The foyer of the theatre, where guided tours begin, also gives access to the Exhibition Hall and the library and patrons are invited to visit these areas before or after their tour. There is also a coffee shop in the foyer and showcases where memorabilia from the theatre archives are displayed.

The building's smallest theatre, the Recording Hall, is also at ground level. Tucked away between the Cinema and the Drama Theatre, it seats three hundred. This auditorium is equipped with all the facilities necessary to produce commercial recordings but as most artists and orchestras, including the Sydney Symphony Orchestra, prefer to record in the Concert Hall, where the acoustics are considered among the world's best, the Recording Hall is used most often for chamber music concerts, dance and drama, and as an extra rehearsal studio.

The Recording Hall, Cinema, Library and Exhibition Hall came into being as a result of the interior design changes of 1967. This area, below the Concert Hall in which they now stand, was originally intended to house stage machinery and a scenery dock for that theatre. These facilities were to have been similar to those which serve the Opera Theatre. While producers and designers continue to lament the fact that the Concert Hall is without these facilities, their consolation is that more opportunities for audiences and artists were made possible with the creation of further venues that now stand where the stage machinery and scenery dock were envisaged.

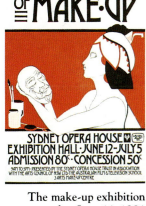

The make-up exhibition was opened on June 11, 1981 by Sir Robert Helpmann, who was then 72. He said he envied the young artists of today who are benefiting from the tremendous advances in the field of make-up. 'Think of the miracles that have been created with Latex!' he marvelled.

The Playmaking exhibition was presented by the Old Tote Theatre Company and the Sydney Opera House Trust in August 1976.

SEEN AND UNSEEN

The Opera House at work

The tiles which cover the sail roofs are constantly checked for wear and tear.

Left. From the shining precipice of the sails, busy craft on the waters below speed down the harbour.

The ceramic tiles which cover the sail roofs of the Opera House are described as "self-cleaning". In fact it is Sydney's showers and particularly the city's tropical rainstorms that keep the sloping roofs looking fresh and sparkling. The tiles were made in Sweden and about one million and fifty-six thousand were needed to cover the roofs. All the tiles look white in photographs, but half of them are actually cream. The cream tiles, which are oblong in shape, have a matt finish and the white tiles, which are glazed, are square.

Narrow exterior "ridge beams" run down the spines of the sail roofs. By walking up and down these "ridge beams" or "ski-runs", which are less than a metre wide, maintenance workers can scan the roofs to see that all the tiles remain smoothly and firmly in place. Spare tiles are held in reserve and when a cracked or loose tile is spotted, a maintenance man in a "bosun's chair" is lowered from one of the "ski-runs" over the billowing slopes to replace it. No doubt business at the Opera House box office would be affected if men were frequently to be seen hovering aloft in bosun's chairs. They are not. Only five roof tiles have had to be replaced during the last ten years. The exterior "ridge beams" or "ski-runs" are reached via a series of interior lofts, tunnels and man-holes. The trek to the summit of the highest sail roof, covering the Concert Hall and sixty-seven metres above sea level, takes about an hour. Anyone undertaking the journey to the roof summits must have a miner's ability to scramble, bent double, along narrow interior passageways. Mountaineering experience would also be an advantage and a head for heights is essential. Because of the difficulties and dangers of the ascent, the management does not encourage visits to "the slopes", but press photographers are occasionally allowed to accompany maintenance men to the peaks, providing they sign papers accepting full liability in case of accident.

Steel railings run down either side of the exterior "ridge beams". From far below, the railings look like hand-rails, but they are, in fact, lightning conductors. At less than a metre high they are too low-slung to serve adequately as hand-rails, although they are used as such by

The glass which lets light flood the foyers is subject to wind and rain, and the smog of a great city. Cleaning these transparent walls is a perpetual occupation.

crouching maintenance workers. The main safety advantage of the railings, however, is that they provide an anchorage to which the men's safety harnesses can be clipped. The supple railings are not strong enough to bear the weight of workmen lowered down over the billowing sail roofs, with their tools, to carry out repair work. Wooden pulleys which are firmly embedded at intervals down the length of the concrete "ski-runs" provide moorings for that purpose.

There are no sheer drops from the peaks of the Opera House to the promenade or glass canopied foyers below. Anyone not wearing a safety harness who toppled from the "ski-runs" would be confronted by a blood-curdling slippery dip slide to disaster over the billowing roofs. Maintenance workers say that the main hazard in balancing on the "ski slopes" is the buffeting winds — not the distraction of the magnificent panorama. No matter how serene the weather below, blustery conditions are always reported from the roof tops.

The Opera House's team of two hundred and ninety permanent staff includes the seventy-five members of the Services Engineer's Department who are responsible for roof maintenance and other maintenance work throughout the complex. One of the regular tasks of this department is to check the twenty thousand light fittings. About fifteen thousand, five hundred lamps or light bulbs have to be changed annually at the Opera House, even down to those which frame the mirrors in the artists' dressing-rooms. The Engineer's staff are also responsible for ensuring that it's "all systems go", for electrical work, carpentry, re-painting, re-carpeting and other refurbishing and repairs as necessary. It is the aid of "Services Engineer's" — always on call — which is sought when the drama company's wardrobe mistress is having trouble with a backstage washing machine, or the chef demands a new stove, or the general manager wants a cartoon framed for his office, or somebody locks a cupboard and loses the key. The department's air-conditioning engineers, who work in shifts around the clock, sit like submariners in plant rooms below ground, monitoring huge cooling and heating systems and checking "digital readouts" informing them of temperature and humidity levels. The normal temperature throughout the building is twenty-two and a half degrees Celsius — seventy-two degrees Fahrenheit — with fifty-two percent humidity but adjustments in specific areas can be made on request. For example, dancers in a rehearsal studio may ask for the temperature there to be lowered after they have spent a strenuous half-hour in class. In the winter, patrons often ask for the air-conditioning to be adjusted — especially if they are wearing heavy woollen clothing and have been applauding enthusiastically. Most requests for air-conditioning adjustments, however, are received in the control room during the summer when theatre patrons in flimsy dresses and lightweight suits walk out of very hot and humid

An interior tunnel makes it possible for service staff to reach the summits of the sails. Like standing on a concrete mountain, their descent by foot is guided by the lightning conductor ready to hand.

Many of the interior corridors are not only thoroughfares for a cast of thousands but carry lifelines of power, water supply and air-conditioning to every part of the complex.

Late afternoon beneath the monumental steps. Here the entrances to Box Office, Stage Door, the Concert Hall, the Opera Theatre and the Bennelong Restaurant await the expectant rush in an hour or two.

conditions into the comparative cool of the theatres. The Opera House's air-conditioning experts say the most difficult task in the world is finding a temperature which pleases everyone. They advise theatre patrons to cloak heavy top coats, wraps and sweaters during the winter and to bring light wraps or jackets into the theatre with them during the summer.

The building's electrical wiring, air-conditioning and plumbing pipes — many of the latter as gargantuan as prehistoric monsters — coil their way from the bowels of the complex, below sea-level, to the very summits of the sail roofs. Most of these veins and blood vessels and organs are hidden from sight behind walls, below floors and above ceilings, but some pipes and ducts, many of them wrapped in silver insulating foil, are visible overhead in the maze of interior corridors. During backstage tours there are lighting, sound and broadcaster's booths to be inspected in the theatres and the control panels operated by the stage managers. The telephones in the wings never ring — no one on stage or in the theatre wants to be distracted by the sound of a telephone — a small red light on the handset flashes on and off to attract attention to a caller waiting on the line. It may be a theatre manager who wants to ask the stage manager to hold the curtain for five minutes because the conductor or the Park & Ride buses are running late. Mishaps do occur.

The first aid room is ready for many emergencies and has qualified nurses always on call.

There is a scenery dock at ground level. Sets are brought from the dock to the Opera Theatre — two levels above — on two transport platforms which form part of the floor at the rear of the stage. Between acts, when one or both of the transport platforms are being loaded or unloaded with scenery at ground level, a safety net is secured across the wide gap left in the floor. If an unwary visitor did fall, literally through the floor, before the safety net was in place, he might plummet two levels to doom — or be lucky — and drop only a metre or so onto one of the platforms as it was returning, unloaded, to form part of the floor. Two similar transport platforms are incorporated in the Opera Theatre's stage revolve. The platforms can be used for effect, as well as floor space and transportation. The illusion of canals, lakes and dungeons can be created by varying the levels at which various sections of the stage floor are held by mechanical means.

When drama and concerts are presented in the Opera Theatre the floor of the orchestral pit can be raised to stage level to form an "apron" — or additional area of forestage. The transport platforms are operated from electrically powered consoles located in the wings, at ground level and in the galleries above the stage. Backdrops are raised and lowered from the "flies" with electrically-powered or hand-operated winches in the galleries above the stage. The Opera Theatre's sophisticated stage machinery is the envy of its neighbour, the Concert Hall, where backdrops and scenes are mounted entirely by manpower. Backstage in the Concert Hall there is an orchestral assembly area — like a carpeted waiting room with mirrors — and a stage manager's control desk in the wings. No transport platforms form part of the stage. Musician's stands and chairs and the grand piano for concerts are brought to the orchestral assembly area in a goods lift from storage rooms below ground.

Right. The lift underneath the Opera Theatre stage rises from its vast well to the level of the auditorium far above. Stage hands steady the sets for La Boheme.

Scenery shifters, stage managers, sound and lighting masters and film projectionists are part of the technical manager's staff of seventy-five. This team, working in shifts, and sometimes supplemented by 'casuals' prepares the stages for all rehearsals, performances and conventions. Technical staff also bring catwalks, lecterns, microphones, trestle tables and chairs to the foyers for receptions, fashion parades and meetings, and they set up stages and dance floors and public address systems for the attractions outdoors. They also tune the Opera House's ten grand and twelve upright pianos and the Hammond X66 organ and investigate new theatrical technology for the building.

The main theatres and the Bennelong Restaurant, which lies beneath the smallest set of sail roofs, can be reached from outside by the staircase or from entrances on the concourse — the long tunnel that runs under the monumental steps. The stage door is also reached from the concourse.

Stagehands in the Drama Theatre prepare the ingenious sets for Congreve's Way of the World which the 'revolve' will change for each new scene.

Right. The Stage Door is manned by members of the security staff who keep every part of the building under careful surveillance. Television monitors facilitate this and an intricate alarm system gives immediate warning of any danger or malfunction.

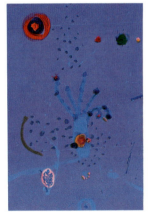

A bright, intriguing detail from Olsen's mural, Salute to Five Bells. Its subject is the harbour and the poet's friendship with Joe Lynch drowned in its waters.

Concrete ribbing underneath the sail roofs has its own pragmatic patterns and carries the stress with inanimate aplomb.

Everyone with business backstage enters the Opera House through the stage door. The office there is the building's communications centre — a place where messages, telegrams and bouquets are left for delivery. The stage door office also serves as the building's crisis centre in an emergency. Consoles give warning of fire or forced entry and point out the location of the danger. If trouble is indicated, the firemen and security officers based at the stage door inform patrolling colleagues to take action. Communication is by two-way radio. The Opera House has an automatic sprinkler system and other fire-fighting equipment is strategically placed around the building. In case of fire, the stage door indicator board will also activate alarms at fire brigade headquarters in the city. When candles are used as props on stage during operas and plays, one of the Opera House's firemen is always on duty in the wings. During a performance of Puccini's Tosca in 1981 candles ignited a backdrop — but the quick thinking of the bass-baritone, John Shaw, who threw a glass of wine onto the fire and the almost simultaneous action of a fireman, who doused the flickering flames from behind the scenes, enabled the performance to proceed virtually uninterrupted.

Security staff and firemen are part of the House Services' Department — which has fifty members, including a team of three nursing sisters who provide first aid for patrons, artists and staff. They have a direct line to Sydney Hospital, about a kilometre away. Most members of the department work in shifts around the clock. Their tasks include looking after lost children, administering the lost property office, directing traffic in the forecourt, issuing identity cards and helping to protect visiting royalty and heads of state.

The stage door leads onto the 'central passageway', a wide interior corridor which runs the length of the Opera House at ground level. Semi-trailers are admitted through tilting doors at either end of the passage to deliver and pick up scenery and props. All the backstage corridors and stairs lead to the Green Room, a capacious gathering place set above the central passageway and the ground floor theatres and lying below the major theatres and foyers.

Artists, staff and company administrators can entertain their guests in the Green Room, where there is a canteen, bar and a lounge looking out onto the harbour, but the public and press are not admitted. Artists wander in from their dressing rooms in bathrobes and kimonos, and during dress rehearsals the line-up for lunch is one of the most entertaining and informative spectacles at the Opera House. One glance at the canteen queue gives a good idea of forthcoming attractions. It may feature the prima donna as Verdi's Lady Macbeth, stage

The steps beside the Concert Hall have ceilings of wooden vaulting — stone, glass and wood distinguish these interior stairways and contrast dramatically with the pristine exterior image of the building.

Right. The Green Room caters for the inner man and woman, it is a place of relaxation and looks out onto the passing harbour scene through a window housed between the two main halls. Inquisitive tourists ascending the stairs outside never suspect they are observed.

hands in shorts and jeans, opera chorus members dressed as witches, with the visiting pianist sandwiched between. There will be accountants and administrators direct from the boardroom, baritones as courtiers in doublet and hose, somebody's mother, very much amused, and dancers in practice tights direct from class — or straight from rehearsal dressed as jesters and elves. Performances and rehearsals can be watched in the Green Room on closed-circuit television and the stage manager's announcements are broadcast to the Green Room as well as the dressing rooms: 'Members of the orchestra, your five-minute call. Five minutes please.' 'Dame Joan, your ten-minute call. Ten minutes please.' 'Clifford Grant's dresser, Mr Grant's dresser. Please report to the stage manager's desk. Immediately please.' These summonses to the wings are always announced calmly, but what 'butterflies' they must often set afluttering!

APPENDIX

Essential Statistics

About the building...

The Opera House covers approximately 1.82 hectares (4½ acres) of its 2.23 hectare (5½ acre) peninsular site, Bennelong Point, on Sydney Harbour.

The complex is approximately 183 metres (200 yards) long and 118 metres (120 yards) wide – at its widest point. The highest shell roof is 67 metres (221 feet) above sea level. The 'sail' roofs are made from 2,194 concrete sections. These sections weigh up to 15.3 tonnes (15 tons). They are held together by 350 kilometres (217 miles) of tensioned cable. More than 1,056,000 Swedish-made ceramic tiles in white and cream cover the concrete roofs.

The weight of the roofs totals 160,956 tonnes (157,800 tons). The roofs are supported on 580 concrete columns, many of which are embedded at rock bottom in Sydney Harbour. The exterior (and many interior) walls, stairs and floors are faced with beige aggregate granite, which was quarried at Tarana in New South Wales.

6,223 square metres (67,000 square feet) of glass, made in France, was required to fill in the mouths of the 'sail' roofs and other areas of the building. The glass is of double thickness. One layer is clear, the other topaz tinted. About 2,000 panes of glass in 700 different sizes were installed during construction.

Diary of construction

Stage 1: Building of the foundations and base to podium level by Civil and Civic Pty Ltd from 1959 to 1963.
Stage 11: Construction of the 'sail' roofs by The Hornibrook Group Pty Ltd from 1963 to 1967.
Stage 111: Installation of glass and construction of the interiors, promenade and approaches by The Hornibrook Group Pty Ltd from 1967 to 1973.

Architects

Stages 1 and 11: Jørn Utzon.
Stage 111: E.H. Farmer, Peter Hall, Lionel Todd and David Littlemore.

Civil engineers

Ove Arup & Partners.

Management

A board of directors, the Sydney Opera House Trust, was established by the New South Wales Government to administer the Opera House as a performing arts centre as early as 1961 – 12 years before the complex opened for performances. Chairmen of the trust have included: Sir Stanley Haviland (1961-1969), Sir Philip Baxter (1969-1975), Mr F.S. Buckley, OBE (1975-1977), Sir Robert Norman (1977-1981) and David Block, the current chairman, who has been head of the trust since 1981.

General managers

Stuart Bacon (1967-1973).
Frank Barnes (1973-1978).
Lloyd Martin, who has been been general manager since 1978 joined the staff of the Opera House as deputy general manager in 1973.

Bennelong Club

The Opera House's Bennelong Club is for young people under 30 who are interested in the performing arts and life at the Opera House. The club arranges meetings with artists, visits to rehearsals and performances, and parties and dances for members and their guests. Membership costs $5 a year, or $3 for students. Associate membership for people over 30: $5. Enquiries: Secretary, Bennelong Club, Sydney Opera House, GPO Box 4274, Sydney, 2001.

General information

Postal address: Sydney Opera House, GPO Box 4274, Sydney.
New South Wales, Australia, 2001.
Telephone: (02) 20588.
Telex: SOHT AA 25525.
Telegraphic and cable address: SYDOPHOUSE

Advance programme information:

Available from the Sydney Opera House Publicity Department at the above address, or from most Australian government offices and airlines.
Box Office: The Box Office is open seven days a week. Mail, over-the-counter, telephone, telex and cable bookings are accepted. Holders of all major credit cards can book by telephone between 9 am and 8.30 pm, Monday to Saturday, and between 9 am and 5 pm on Sunday. Call (02) 2 0588 and ask for the 'Instant Charge' service. Telephone orders can be picked up immediately prior to the performance, or mailed if time permits.

Mail orders should be sent to: Box Office Manager, Sydney Opera House, Post Office Box R239, Royal Exchange, Sydney, 2000. If you would like your mail, telex or cabled orders charged, please state type, number and expiry date of your credit card. Alternatively, please enclose cheque or bank draft for the exact value of the tickets ordered.

Package tours for visitors to Sydney:

'An Evening at the Sydney Opera House' is a package which includes a guided tour of the building, a visit to an Opera House exhibition, dinner with wine at the main restaurant, the Bennelong and a ticket to a performance. The inclusive cost ranges from $32.50 to $68 a person, depending on choice of performance. The Opera House's Tourism and Marketing Department also offers a 'Harbourside Sydney in a day' package, which includes a morning coffee cruise on Sydney Harbour, lunch at the Bennelong, and a guided tour of the building. The inclusive cost is $24.50 a person.

For bookings and further information: Tourism and Marketing Department, Sydney Opera Houses, GPO Box 4274, Sydney, 2001. Package tours can be booked up to a year in advance.

Guided tours: Tours of theatres and other front of house areas are conducted continuously between 9 am and 4 pm on every day except Christmas Day and Good Friday. Each tour is of about an hour's duration. Tickets: $2.50 or $1.20 for Australian pensioners, students of any nationality and children. No advance booking necessary, except for parties of 20 or more, or for private tours for one person or a small group. Private tours cost $60. For further information call (02) 2 0588 or write to: Chief Guide, Sydney Opera House, GPO Box 4274, Sydney, 2001. **90 minute backstage tours** are conducted on Sundays between 9 am and 4 pm. Tickets: $5. No advance booking necessary.

Restaurants: The main restaurant, the Bennelong Restaurant, is open for: **Lunch (a la carte)** Monday to Saturday between noon and 2.30 pm. **Business lunch** Monday to Friday between noon and 2.30 pm. **Pre-theatre dinner** Monday to Saturday from 5.30 pm to 7.30 pm.

Dinner (a la carte) – (last orders 10.45 pm) Monday to Saturday from 8 pm. Booking is recommended, especially for pre-theatre dinner. Telephone((02) 20588. Free parking on site is available for patrons with lunch reservations at the Bennelong Restaurant. Reserve parking when booking your table.

The self-service **Harbour Restaurant** on the promenade is open seven days a week from 11 am to 8 pm. Meals, snacks and take-away food are served.

Latecomers: Please be on time for performances. Latecomers are not admitted until there is a break in the programme. **Disabled patrons:** Facilities and services for the disabled include free parking on site, wheelchair service if required and escorted elevator service to and from theatre seats. Disabled patrons are requested to book parking space in advance in office hours. Call the House Service Department on (02) 20588. A leaflet for the disabled will be mailed on request.

Library: The Opera House's Dennis Wolanski Library and Archives of the Performing Arts is open from 9 am to 5 pm, Monday to Friday. The Library houses an extensive collection of scores, libretti, catalogues, books, newspapers and magazines on the performing arts. The assistance of staff is available, without charge, to researchers and the general public. A coffee bar adjoins the reading room. The library was established in 1973 with the help of a grant of $10,000 from the Sydney businessman and sculptor, Dennis Wolanski. The Ladies Committee of the Sydney Opera House Appeal Fund has since raised tens of thousands of dollars to help stock the libray and maintain the archives. Volunteer workers help maintain the library's extensive collection of reviews and press clippings but donations of theatre memorabilia are always being sought.

For further information please contact the librarian, Paul Bentley, Sydney Opera House, GPO Box 4274, Sydney, 2001. Telephone: (02) 20588.

Conventions, receptions, parties: A wide variety of social and public events are regularly catered for at the Opera House. Convention facilities include multilingual translation systems for up to five languages. For further information contact the Catering Manager, Sydney Opera House, GPO Box 4274, Sydney, 2001. Telephone: (02) 20588. Telex: SOHT AA 25525. Telegraphic: SYDOPHOUSE.

Hire of theatres for performances: Contact the Theatre Lettings Manager, at the above address.

Theatres – seating capacities

Concert Hall: Maximum of 2,690.

Opera Theatre: Maximum of 1,547, but 98 box seats have a restricted to severely restricted view of the stage.

Drama Theatre: Maximum of 544.

Cinema: Maximum of 419.

Recording Hall: Maximum of 300.

Reception Hall: Accommodates maximum of 200.

Technical information for entrepreneurs: Comprehensive, printed information about stage measurements and the technical facilities available in all the complex's theatres is available on request from the technical director, Sydney Opera House, GPO Box 4274, Sydney, 2001.

Appearances for the Sydney Opera House Trust:
Artists and managements seeking engagements by the Sydney Opera House Trust should contact the Concert Manager, at the above address.

Addresses of major hirers of Opera House theatres – please contact these companies direct regarding season tickets, auditions and engagements:

The Australian Opera
15th Floor,
AMP Building,
Corner Bridge and Phillip Streets,
Sydney, 2001
Telephone: (02) 231 2300

The Australian Ballet
11 Mount Alexander Road,
Flemington, Vic. 3031.
Telephone: (03) 376 1400
Telex: AUSBAL AA 35905

Sydney Theatre Company
153 Dowling Street,
Potts Point, 2011
Telephone: (02) 358 4399

Telex: EXSTCE AA 73209

ABC Concerts
Australian Broadcasting Corporation,
GPO Box 487,
Sydney, 2001
Telephone: (02) 339 0211
Telex: ABCOM AA 26506

Musica Viva Australia
68-70 Clarence Street,
Sydney, 2000
Telephone: 29 8165
Telex: MUSICAVIV AA 70239

Sydney Dance Company
36 Bourke Street,
Woolloomooloo, 2011
Telephone: (02) 358 4600

Marionette Theatre of Australia
Australia's National Puppet Theatre
The Sailors Home Building,
106-108 George Street Nth.,
Sydney, 2000
Telephone: (02) 241 1391

Acknowledgements

Paul Bentley and Ralph Bott, Dennis Wolanksi Library and Archives of the Performing Arts, Sydney Opera House; Paul Hammond, Librarian; the Australian Ballet;

Shirley Humphries and Christine Pryke, Mitchell Library, State Library of New South Wales; Sotheby's Australia Pty Ltd; Royal Australian Historical Society; John Ferguson Pty Ltd Publishers; Australian Information Service; Government House, Sydney; Government House, Canberra; New South Wales Government Printing Office; National Library, Canberra; John Fairfax and Sons; News Limited; The Hon E. G. Whitlam; Sir Charles Moses; Miss Betty Cook; Ewart Chappel; Margaret Carter and Hildegarde Rule, ABC Concerts; Carol McPhee and Carmel Dalco, The Australian Opera; Rae de Teliga, Musica Viva Australia; Sydney Dance Company; Australian Film Institute; Elizabeth Butcher, National Institute of Dramatic Art; Anne Churchill-Brown, Sydney Theatre Company; The Marionette Theatre of Australia – Australia's National Puppet Theatre; Dick Hoole and Jack McCoy Films; David Brown, Sydney Opera House Publicity Department; John Nutt, Ove Arup and Partners; Michael Edgley International Pty Ltd.

Photographic Credits

Don McMurdo, Sydney Opera House; **Ray Joyce,** Lansdowne Press; **Reg Morrison,** Lansdowne Press.

Max Dupain; Gordon Clarke; Dennis Delfavero; Robert Walker; Alex J. Langley; Miki Kamatsu; Tommy Casiano; TCN Channel 9; Branco Gaica.

INDEX

An Index of Significant Names, Events and Performances